NOTES FOR THE NILE

A rich account of Egyptian archaeology and the hymns of ancient Egypt, this book is at once a fascinating textbook and a practical guide. Readers with a background in Egyptology as well as those just beginning will be delighted by H. D. Rawnsley's disarming style and often-amusing advice: "On no pretext be induced to drink Nile water," "If you find a donkey falls, change him; he will do it again," "One often escapes the importunity of those who ask for 'bakhsheesh' by nodding, and saying with a smile, 'Boókra,' which means 'To-morrow.'"

NOTES FOR THE NILE

TOGETHER WITH A METRICAL RENDERING OF THE HYMNS OF
ANCIENT EGYPT AND OF THE PRECEPTS OF PTAH-HOTEP

BY
HARDWICKE D. RAWNSLEY

Routledge
Taylor & Francis Group
LONDON AND NEW YORK

First published in 1892 by Heinemann.

This edition first published in 2009 by
Routledge
2 Park Square, Milton Park, Abingdon, Oxon, OX14 4RN

Simultaneously published in the USA and Canada
by Routledge
711 Third Avenue, New York, NY 10017

Routledge is an imprint of the Taylor & Francis Group, an informa business

© Heinemann 1892

First issued in paperback 2012

British Library Cataloguing in Publication Data
A catalogue record for this book is available from the British Library

ISBN13: 978-0-7103-0983-9 (hbk)

ISBN13: 978-0-415-65576-7 (pbk)

Publisher's Note
The publisher has gone to great lengths to ensure the quality of this reprint
but points out that some imperfections in the original copies may be
apparent. The publisher has made every effort to contact original copyright
holders and would welcome correspondence from those they have been
unable to trace.

A RETURN TO EGYPT

There is a land where Time no count can keep,
 Where works of men imperishable seem;
 Where through death's barren solitude doth gleam
Undying hope for them that sow and reap :
Yea, land of life where death is but a deep
 Warm slumber, a communicable dream,
 Where from the silent grave far voices stream
Of those who tell their secrets in their sleep.

Land of the palm-tree and the pyramid,
 Land of sweet waters from a mystic urn,
 Land of sure rest where suns shine on for ever,
I left thee—in thy sands a heart was hid,
 My life, my love, were cast upon thy river,
 And, lo ! to seek Osiris I return.

H. D. R.

CONTENTS

CONTENTS

INTRODUCTION

PRECEPTS FOR TRAVELLERS

This book ends with precepts for people in Egypt, from the oldest book in the world, B.C. 3666.

It shall begin with precepts for travellers in Egypt in the year A.D. 1892.

Three journeys to the East make one feel that guide-books are not sufficiently explicit as to such details as are here given, and this must be my apology for venturing to give the following bits of advice.

1. As to dress. Dress as you would in England in early summer, but take a good wrap: flannel shirts and flannel belt; mornings and evenings are often chilly. Wear boots rather than shoes, because there are such things as asps in Egypt; and brown rather than black, because of the heat. Cream for cleaning these boots, should be taken out from England, as it is not always procurable abroad, and if not used, the boots are soon spoiled by the dry hot sand. Canvas leggings for men, and a light serge skirt (walking length) for ladies, are advisable, because donkeys are dirty and tombs are dusty. Wear a sun helmet, or (better) a

soft, grey felt ıde-awake, double thickness. Take a strong white ͺnglish-made umbrella, lined with green or blue, and a pair of glasses—smoked, not blue—for use when riding over desert-sand.

2. As to food, everything can be got in Cairo, except good English tea. On no pretext be induced to drink Nile water, when at anchor; avoid it at all times, unless boiled. The Nile is the drain of all Egypt. Dwellers on the banks of it know that it contains a parasite which is a troublesome customer, if it takes up its abode in the human body. Light claret and St. Galmier and other mineral waters can be obtained for you by Gaze or Cook. Never let flies settle on your face; they may bring ophthalmia. Use lotion at the first symptom.

3. Medicines. Pyretic saline, quinine, Dover's powder (these last in the form of pills), chlorodyne, a roll of plaster, lint, a bit of oil-silk, a box of mustard leaves, compound colocynth pills, an eye-douche and eye-lotion obtained in Cairo, are all that is necessary. For use amongst natives, a box of eye ointment (red oxide of mercury). Good doctors are at Luxor and on the Nile steamers; and in case of typhoid, most devoted nursing, with the best possible medical skill, can be obtained at the German Deaconesses' Hospital in Cairo. If ill, do not stay in the hotel, but remove at once, under doctor's orders, to the hospital.

4. Take a reel of magnesium wire; there is great difficulty in obtaining a satisfactory lamp for the continuous burning of magnesium wire. Procure a tin reflector, like a stable lantern, to hold five candles, with socket and long stick. This enables the traveller to see the more interesting drawings and sculptures, which are generally best preserved on the upper parts of tombs and temples.

Good writing and drawing materials, note-books, &c., are not obtainable in Cairo.

The little " Kodak " camera is very useful for instantaneous photographs of figures, &c.

5. Donkeys. In Cairo, engage and pay for your donkeys through the hotel porter. Examine for raw place under broad belt and under tail, before engaging. If you find a donkey falls, change him ; he will do it again. On going up Nile, see the ladies' saddles, and have them marked before leaving, or you may be put off with native-made instead of English-made saddles, which are often unusable, and the straps of which are generally rotten. See that your side-saddles, are not whisked off from your steamer, as you return, on to another steamer passing up.

6. Dragomen. However well recommended, never expect your dragoman to know anything about Egyptian history or the monuments up Nile. Go, knowing what you want to see, and insist on seeing it. Refuse to allow your dragoman to take " a squeeze "

for you from any of the monuments. He is generally very ready to do so, and much damage has been done in this way.

In Cairo it will save you time and expense to engage a dragoman for the day. He knows the mosques best worth seeing, and can get all the necessary orders, and will easily save you his day's pay at the bazaars.

7. In dealing with the people, treat them as gentlemen. The Eastern, who is always polite, appreciates this. He understands a joke also. One often escapes the importunity of those who ask for " bakhsheesh " by nodding, and saying with a smile, " Boókra," which means "To-morrow." Above all things, remember the religion of Muhammad is a real thing in Egypt. Show deference to religious belief and custom, and a becoming reverence when you enter any of their mosques. To avoid missing interesting scenes, ascertain the days of religious festivals.

8. If you want to see the monuments, remember that this cannot possibly be done in a crowd. Travellers by small steamer or dahabîeh will have the best of it in this matter.

It is well to ask if there is any peasant in the neighbourhood, who has been in the employ of one or other of the explorers of late years. These men have exact memories, and can often point out to you objects of interest that you would otherwise miss. Make a public example of any one in your company you catch defacing a monument, either by scribbling his name or by taking fragments of it away. Posterity will bless you.

9. As to scarabs, never purchase, except at the Gîzeh Museum, unless you are an expert. Nineteen out of twenty, offered for sale up Nile, were manufactured in the scarab-makers' shops, and buried or worn next to the skin by the vendor, to give the appearance of age, and colour.

As to papyri, do not refuse a portion of one—it may contain a valuable text. If you obtain possession of one that has not been unrolled, do not attempt to unroll it, or allow the man from whom you buy it to do so ; but take it to your national museum, let the authorities examine it, and if important, leave it with them. It is necessary to allow scholars of the Egyptian language the fullest possible access to any texts that are discovered.

10. It will save you much perplexity, and add to the pleasure of the Nile voyage, if you have made yourself familiar, beforehand, with the main historical facts and characteristics of the various epochs and dynasties ; if you know the cartouches of the more important kings ; and if the leading features and symbols of the ancient Egyptian religion and divinities, the localities of the various gods, and the general arrangement of temple worship, are grasped. For this latter, see Mariette

Bey's "Monuments of Upper Egypt," pp. 38 and 127. By no means fail to take this last passage in your hand when visiting the temple of Denderah.

The best books for those who would study the Egyptian monuments and history are the Egyptian collections in the various national museums. Travellers, before starting for the Nile, should, if possible, have visited the British Museum and the Louvre, and before sailing up river, should make a point of spending some considerable time in the Gîzeh Museum.

11. Books to be read before going to Egypt:— Brugsch Bey's "Egypt under the Pharaohs," last edition; G. Maspero's "Histoire Ancien des Peuples de l'Orient"; Page Renouf's "Hibbert Lectures," 1879; "Records of the Past," Series I. and II. (Bagster); Wilkinson's "Ancient Egyptians"; Lane's "Modern Egyptians"; Stuart Poole's "Cities of Egypt"; S. Birch's "Ancient History from the Monuments"; Wallis Budge's "The Dwellers on the Nile"; Professor Rawlinson's "Ancient Egypt" in the Story of the Nations Series; Villiers Stuart's "Nile Gleanings"; Berkley's "The Pharaohs and their People"; Miss Edwards' "A Thousand Miles up the Nile"; Ebers' "Egypt Illustrated"; "The History of Ancient Egyptian Art," by Perrot and Chipiez; "The Egyptian Exploration Fund Transactions"; and anything that Mr. Flinders Petrie has written on Egypt.

Books to be taken out to Egypt:—Baedeker's

" Lower Egypt," for Cairo, Pyramids, and Sakkarah ; Murray's " Egypt," last edition, for up Nile ; Wallis Budge's " The Nile " (this admirable handbook is the property of Messrs. Cook & Son, and not obtainable from the booksellers); Mariette Bey's " Outlines of Ancient Egyptian History " ; " Mariette Bey's " The Monuments of Upper Egypt."

I wish here to express my personal indebtedness to the writers of all these books for the help they have accorded me.

HARDWICKE D. RAWNSLEY.

NOTES FOR THE NILE

CHAPTER I.

ON TOMBS.

EGYPTIAN HISTORY proper begins with the reign of King M'na, Mena, or Menes, the first king of the first dynasty. Before his time all is legend, and the legend takes the form of the assertion that Egypt was governed first by divinities, then by heroes, part man part god.

But Mena is no mythical person. He was the first overlord or tribal king who in his person united several petty chieftains of the then inhabitants of the land of Nile—the dark men whose skin was of the colour of the crocodile (*kam*), and the soil of whose fields (the land of Ham) was dark as the colour of their hands.

Whether or not he came as a conqueror from Mesopotamia, and moving from This or Thinis, near

A

Abydos,* set up his capital at the "Haven of the Good" (Menefer or Memphis of to-day), and constructed a gigantic dam to turn aside the river Nile from its bed, and give him the security of fields, encircled by its silver arm of defence, is conjectural.

This much we may be pretty certain of, that Mena reigned not later than 4400 B.C. (Brugsch), perhaps as early as 5004 B.C. (Mariette), and was the founder of the ancient empire.

For convenience' sake, Egyptian history, the history of the thirty-one dynasties of rulers, is divided into three periods—the Ancient, the Middle, the New Empires.

The Ancient Empire includes the first eleven dynasties, and, if we accept Mariette's date, lasted 1940 years ; if we accept Brugsch's date, it lasted from 4400 B.C. to 2500 B.C.—that is, 1900 years ; a longer time, as both of these writers agree, than the Christian era.

The Middle Empire includes the next nine dynasties, the twelfth up to the twentieth inclusive, from 2466 B.C. to 1200 B.C. The New Empire includes the remaining ten dynasties, and lasts from 1200 B.C. to 360 B.C. After Nectanebo, the last of the Egyptian kings, came the Persians, to be followed by the Macedonians under Alexander the Great in 332 B.C., by the Ptolemies in 305 B.C., and by the Romans in 27 B.C.

---

* It has been suggested of late that the modern Girgeh may be the site of ancient This.

We shall deal in this chapter chiefly with funeral monuments of the Ancient Empire, and shall only introduce tomb monuments of a later period for illustration's sake.

The belief in the persistence of life after death is discovered in all religions. Ancestor-worship, or the desire to offer propitiatory offerings to the manes of the dead, is seen in the "Inferiæ" and "Parentalia" of Rome, and in the "Enagismata" of the Greeks. When we turn to Indo-European nations, we find the Hindu worshipping the "Pitris," and the Iranians believing in a kind of disembodied spirit of the dead, called "Fravashi"; while, turning to China, we note there that the oldest institution of the oldest civilisation now extant is the celebration of rites in honour of defunct ancestors.*

It may or may not be true, as according to Mr. Herbert Spencer, that the rudimentary form in all religion is the propitiation of dead ancestors; but it is certain that, as far as Egypt goes, this belief had been already superseded by a very different set of notions as long ago as the founding of the pyramids; for the oldest form of prayer extant in that far-off time of advanced Egyptian civilisation which we speak of as the age of the pyramids—3766 B.C. to 3366 B.C. —shows us that the Egyptians, in their most ancient propitiation of ancestors, always made it through

* *Cf.* Page Renouf, "Hibbert Lectures," p. 124.

prayer, not to the ancestor, but to Anubis, Osiris, or some other god; whilst the deceased is described in the funeral inscription as "faithful to the great God."

Diodorus tells us: "The Egyptians call their houses hostelries, on account of the short time during which they inhabit them, but the tombs they call eternal dwelling-places." And this, as Page Renouf points out to us, is literally and entirely true.

In the oldest inscriptions the tomb is described as "Pa t'eta"—eternal dwelling-place; whilst the departed are spoken of as "Anchiu"—that is, "the living ones."

There are in the Egyptian court of the British Museum the fragments of the wooden coffin of Mycerinus or Menkaura, the builder of the third pyramid of Gîzeh, 3633 B.C., and one of the names that is written thereon, to describe the sarcophagus in which the good king was buried, is Neb Anch, which means "The Lord of Life."

That sarcophagus, it is believed, never contained the body of the pious king; but he lives for ever in the praises of Herodotus, for the historian says of him: "That he restored the religious services, opened the temples, made the most just decisions of all the kings; and if a man complained of the decision of the judgment, he made a present to him out of his own treasury, and pacified his anger." This by way of parenthesis, but 'tis passing strange how,

after the lapse of fifty-five centuries, the name of
Mycerinus, good and just, smells sweet, and blossoms
from the desert dust.

But where did the Egyptians stow their sarcophagi,
these coffins that were the "chests of the living," as
they were called?

Rest assured that they would take care to place
them in security if possible, and so, since the Nile
was a great high roadway or high waterway, the
ancients buried their dead, generally, as far from the
Nile banks as they could, and though they did not
always do so, yet they seem to have affected the
western side of the Nile where possible; partly
because, as is the case with the great burial-ground
that stretches from Gîzeh to Dahshûr and the
Mêdûm—from the Pyramid of Abú Roâsh, in the
north, to the Pyramid of Seneferu in the south, the
Nile flowed farthest away from their necropolis, and
enemies and robbers of tombs were least likely to
advance from the barren western desert; and
partly because the great principle of life, the sun,
entered the realm of darkness each day in the west,
and symbolised that sunset of existence here on earth
which the tomb chambers bore witness to.

Sometimes, of course, the Libyan Desert, to the
west, gave no limestone plateau to dig the tombs in,
or raise the pyramid and mastăba on, no good resting
ground for the eternal dwelling-places, and then the

Egyptians sought to the plateau cliff on the eastern side, and, as at Beni hasân, Tel El Amarna and El-Kab, they hewed them sepulchral halls and pits for the burial of their dead in the cliffs of the morning sun.

But when, as happens at Gebel Silsilis, the cliffs come right up on each side to the river, and good substantial rock tombs are obtainable on either side, there we find that the old love of burial in the land of the sunset comes to the front again, and the tomb chambers are hewn only on the western side.

We have spoken of sepulchral halls and pits : what do we mean?

We remember the verse in the psalm, " Our bones lie scattered before the pit, like as when one breaketh and heweth wood upon the earth ;" or again, " Thou hast laid me in the lowest pit, in a place of darkness and in the deep."

We remember the old Hebrew expression of "going down into the pit," and these sayings are but so many reminders that the Hebrews had been dwellers in Egypt, where the abode of eternity, the tomb proper, was always, if possible, placed at the bottom of a deep shaft sunk into the solid rock.

The traveller in Egypt to-day, who enters the tomb of Tih or Ptah-hotep at Sakkâra, the rock grottos at Beni hasân, Tel El Amarna, El-Kab, or Gebel Silsilis, Asyût, or Aswân, has to remember that he is not visiting any tomb proper at all.   These halls and grottos are but the festal meeting-places for friends of the dead, votive and memorial chambers. The dead man, to whose memory they were hewn and decorated, slept in his chamber-tomb at the bottom of the pit, many yards beneath the feet of those who came together to propitiate the gods and feed the dead man's "Ka," or spirit, or genius, or double, and make mention of his name with song and festal pomp on the funeral-feast days.

It is true that the poor men in ancient times were simply wrapped in reed mats, and huddled within the clay—instances of which burial I saw last year near Seneferu's Pyramid; but the man who could afford for his body his bath of brine for seventy days, and his tub of oil and resin and unguents for a like period, and could pay from £60 to £250 for the embalmer's process, took care in life to have a proper house for eternity prepared for his mortal remains. This tomb, under the ancient empire generally, consisted of five parts.

First. A visible mound of sun-burnt brick or stone, which might measure in length and breadth 170 feet by 86 feet, or 36 feet by 20 feet, and might be 13 feet high, which took the form of an oblong and truncated pyramid, and which is called to-day a "mastăba," because it resembles a long low bench or divan in shape, such as the Arabs use in their houses, and call by that name.

The pyramid proper is probably only a natural outgrowth from those early mounds, or mastăbas.

Secondly. There comes an outer chamber, generally on the eastern or northern side, which forms a kind of vestibule to the inner chamber, and which sometimes is built as a portico or a prolongation from the mastăba, as in the tomb of Tih. Sometimes it is, as it were, hewn out of the second skin or outside coating of stone or brick of the mastăba, as may be seen in the Mêdûm necropolis.

Thirdly. We have the important inner, or funeral chamber, wherein at certain times the friends assembled. This chamber was richly adorned with colour and sculpture, and here, under the ancient empire, people saw the dead man brought to life again, as far as art could do it, and superintending, as was his habit in life, the labour of his field, the hunting, the fishing, the boat-building, &c., that he had cared for on earth.

Fourthly. At the further end of this chamber was a recess, walled across, and having generally only a tiny slit in the screen wall for the fumes of incense, used on the memorial days to pass inside. Sometimes even this means of access was closed. This stone recess or cupboard was called the " sirdâb," and in it were placed life-like images of the deceased carved in stone or wood, which might be looked upon as so many media or forms for the Ka, or genius, or spirit, of the departed to enter into and inhabit: so many possibilities of a kind of spirit-possession or re-embodiment for the defunct. In front was generally placed a little offering stool and votive slab. For the sirdâb was the holy of holies of the tomb guest-chamber.

But the important part of the eternal house was the fifth or last part—viz., the pit. This was driven down into the solid rock, sometimes from the antechamber, sometimes from the inner chamber, sometimes from the centre of the mastăba, and hewn of such a size as that a mummy or sarcophagus could be lowered into place. Such a pit shaft is familiar to all who visit Campbell's tomb at Gîzeh.

At the bottom of this pit, 40 or 50 feet deep, was hewn a side passage, generally on the south and east side, that gradually broadened out into a good-sized chamber; the trend of this passage was so arranged as to bring this subterranean chamber exactly under the upper or guest-chamber, where from time to time the friends assembled to pour wine and offer flowers and incense upon the sirdâb, or recess, behind whose wall were hid the images or statues of the departed.

This was the tomb proper; the sarcophagus rested there, and, once lowered down the shaft and taken into its house of eternity, a huge block of stone was lowered into place, to fill the entrance into the passage at the bottom of the well or shaft. The shaft itself was filled up with rubble and sand and stones; and the dead man's body waited for the 3000 years to pass before it should arise from its dust and begin its earthly life again.

In such sanctity of undisturbed repose have many of the Egyptian dead, buried under the ancient empire, remained till this day, that explorers have even found in the soft sand, the tracks of the feet of the bearers who bore the body to its rest in the sub-terranean tomb-chamber, more than 3000 years before Christ.

Of course, when the pyramids arose the ante-chamber and chamber were dispensed with, and friends met in the little temple outside the pyramid to offer prayer and praise and vows in memory of the dead king.

Such a continuity of endowment was allowed to that old Egyptian way of worship, that in the time of the twenty-sixth dynasty we find from a tablet in the Louvre that a priest of Chufu or Cheops, Psamtik by name, is keeping up the memory of Chufu, who built the Great Pyramid and endowed the temple services more than 2000 years before, according to the prescribed ritual of pyramid days, and the pious wishes of the founder. Let the Christian disestab-lishers and disendowers of particular forms of religion, on the ground of emptiness of title after lapse of years, note this.

When we turn away from the mastăbas of the ancient dynasty, and leave the necropolis of Gîzeh and Sakkara, Abusîr, Dahshûr and Mêdûm, for the rock grottos of Beni hasân, Tel El Amarna, El-Kab, Silsilis, Asyût, and Aswân, we find that the ante-chamber has been dispensed with, and we enter beneath a porch, at once, into the Hall of Guests, often splendidly adorned, with its niche, or sirdâb, behind whose partition wall the statues of the defunct were immured, and sometimes in which, perhaps with little more than a low protecting wall between the spectators and themselves, their life-size statues, carved in the living rock, sat to receive the gifts of worshippers.*

Now, what we have to bear in mind is that the tomb

---

* At El-Kab, and also at Aswân, in the tombs opened by Sir W. Grenfell, there were evidences on the ground, of a partition wall which may at one time have entirely screened the statues from sight, but which in the lapse of years had been broken away by the tomb-breakers. It is true that in tombs of the middle or later empire the sirdâb disappears. This may perhaps be accounted for by the fact that the embalmer's process became so perfect that it was not felt necessary to carve any life-size statues for the Ka, or double, or genius, to enter into and inhabit. And it is thought that, with the falling away of this practice of carving statues, another practice may have after obtained—viz., the bringing of the wooden coffin from its rest-chamber to the guest-chamber at stated intervals, or, as is more probable, of having a dummy coffin to use for this purpose on festal days.

proper is not here, but that a pit or shaft has been
sunk deep down into the rock, sometimes as at Asyût
and Beni hasân, from inside the guest-chamber, sometimes, as at El-Kab, from the terrace outside, or from
within the portico to the guest-chamber; and that the
tomb is beneath our feet as we gaze at the mural
decorations of the guest-chamber above.

Occasionally in these guest-chambers is seen a slab
whereon a likeness of the mummy was laid at certain
seasons, or whereon his body was placed for a time,
before it was finally taken down by pit, or sloping
underground passage to its sarcophagus beneath.
Sometimes upon the entrances to this subterranean rest-
chamber are seen bits of the clay seal, still sticking,
which sealed the doorway to the block-fitting, while
clay seals, cones of clay six inches long, have been
found in the sand close by.

What we have still to remember is that we who visit
the tomb of Tih at Sakkara, or the tomb of Ameni,
or Knoum-hotep, to-day at Beni hasân, are really not
in their tombs at all, but only in the guest-chamber
above the tomb, wherein of old time the friends met on
stated occasions, to do honour to the dead man, not yet
out of mind.

The stone sarcophagus and the sarcophagus-chamber
were often unornamented, the latter, if ornamented,
only had lists of festival days and calendars of offerings
upon its walls, such as we see upon the walls of the

tomb of Horhotpou, the son of Sonit-she, a noble who lived at Thebes in the eleventh dynasty, 2500 B.C. Visitors to the Gîzeh Museum will remember that wonderful tomb, with its great calendar of days for offerings, its wall paintings of bows and arrows, of mace and hatchet, of pots of oil and jars of wine, of mirrors, of shoes, of little bags of unguent and henna for the hands, or of kohl powder for the eyes, its pots of seven essences, its green and black paint for face or body; the accessories, in short, of a gentleman's toilet in the last days of the ancient empire, all so necessary to the wellbeing of the Ka, or spirit of Horhotpou, in the world of Amenti, the world beyond the grave, when he came visiting the dead.

The important decoration of these tomb-chambers was lavished on the guest-hall, and, as in the tombs of the kings, upon the long subterranean passages.

But in the guest-chambers of the tombs of the early empire, there is a very great difference in the motive of the ornament, from that which is found in tombs of the middle and new empire. In the tombs of the end of the middle, and beginning of the new empire, it is plain to be seen that the whole idea of the decoration is to set forth the journey of the soul in the next world through all the ordeals it has to go, upon its way to the Hall of Judgment and Justification. The gods are the principals in all these scenes; and the spirit of evil, the serpents spitting fire, the burning fiery furnaces, the crocodiles that open their jaws, are some of the torments the soul must meet with on its way to its eternal rest.

Visitors to the tomb of Seti I. in the Valley of the Kings—Seti whose white sarcophagus this day is seen at Sir John Sloane's Museum—will remember the fiery serpents and the pictured horrors of hell, through which the dead king felt, in his lifetime, he must needs pass, on his way to eternal life.

The men who adorned these guest-chambers evidently felt that the spirit of the dead must pass to purgatory, and prove by its doings in the spirit as well as in the flesh, that it has won the immortality promised, and was fit to be justified in the judgment-hall of Osiris. It should be borne in mind that the guests did not enter these tomb chambers or passages. They met for funeral feast, at some tomb chapel far away. These wall writings were for the study of the king in his lifetime, who prepared his eternal home, and for the reading of the lonely Ka when it came to visit the dead king. Once the body had been borne to its rest, the entrance to the great tomb passage was closed, and hid, if possible, from view.

But in the tomb-guest-chambers of the earlier empire, with which we are dealing now, there was no representation of gods to give judgment, nor of trials to justify. The dead man is represented at home and in peace. His wife is at his side, and holds him tenderly by the arm ; his children are at his feet, or round his knees. The very common attitude of endearment is that the wife or child kneels or squats by the side of the husband or father, and strokes the calf of the good gentleman's leg. He walks abroad to see how the harvest is getting on, he superintends the vintage, gazes at the brickmakers or boat-builders. Dancing girls are before him, and acrobats and wrestlers tumble and wrestle. He goes out hunting the crocodile, or snaring the wild fowl, and when he returns he sits happily in the ancestral chair ; a garland of flowers is on his head, and his wife holds a great lotus lily to his nose for him to smell ; and servants slay the ox, and gather the grapes, and store the honey, and press the wine, and bake the cakes, and cut the sheaves, and bring to him offerings of all flowers and fruits, and give him of the labour of their hands—fish, flesh, fowl, flowers, fruit, beer, wine, "in all manner of abundance, richly to enjoy" ; while the priests, wearing the panther skin and shorn of head, sing and say, "A royal table of propitiation grant Anubis, who dwells in the divine house. May sepulture be granted in the nether world in the land of the divine Amenti, the ancient, the good, the great, to him, the departed, who is faithful to the Great God. May he advance upon the blissful paths upon which those advance who are faithful to the Great God. May the funeral oblations be paid to him at the beginning of the year, at the feasts of the great and of the small heat, at the feasts of each month, and the half-month, and every day," &c. &c. " May his nostrils breathe the north wind, and may he drink of the depth of the river."

Death, if it is hinted at by sight of the funeral-sledge, is at once dismissed. Life is the motive of the wall-sculpture and painting.

Round about the walls are the droves of cattle and asses, and all the operations of the farm are depicted. Little bits of descriptive dialogue are carved above them. For example : " ' This is the killing of the ox.' 'These are the harvestmen.' 'Hold hard,' says a master to his servant. ' Thy will be done,' replies the lad. ' This donkey is wild,' says another. ' I'll tame him,' answers a fourth. ' Beware of the stick,' says a don-key-boy to a recalcitrant donkey. ' Oh, you lazy-bones,' cries a herdsman to the oxen. ' If you bring me eleven thousand and nine stalks of flax, I will comb them,' cries a flax-dresser. ' Make haste, and none of your chatter, you prince of clodhoppers,' replies, somewhat rudely, his fellow-labourer."

Now, what does all this happy pastoral life upon the funeral guest-chamber of the ancient empire mean. Are these people bringing their legs of beef, and geese and ducks, and pigeons and fruits, to offer them as sweet sacrifice to the soul of the departed or to the god for his soul? Are the dancing-girls and tumblers and single-stick players performing a kind of religious tumbling and dancing and play of a sacred propitiatory character? Or is it the faith of the early Egyptians that the world beyond the grave is but a repetition of the world this side of it, and that, if not yet, at least one day, the dead man will wake up and take his old interest in his old life's work, whilst even at this time, before his bodily resurrection, his "Ka" or spirit, or double, is in full sympathy with all that is going on here on earth, and cares as much to see his sons go forth to the harvest, and his daughters bind their brows with flowers, and his servants bring rich produce home from field and river, as ever he did in the days when he saw the great Nile swell out and shine in middle plain, and the green carpet of the corn and lentil change beneath the sun to gleaming gold.

That secret is still a secret of the tomb; the walls tell us much, but they will not cry out yet to tell us more in the way of answer of this question. Egyptologists are still puzzled on this score.

But the chief interest of these funeral guest-chambers centres in this fact of the portraiture of the contemporary life of Egypt.

Not only are we allowed to see how the arts flourish and decay, from the excellence and falling-off in draughtsmanship, in colour, and sculpture, of the wall pictures, but from them we can see the ideals of happy

B

life on earth then, and guess at the fears and hopes of the future world those old Egyptians entertained.

I confess it is rather an eye-opener to find that the art of sculpture in low relief and portraiture, and sense of humour, are at their best in the third, and fourth, and fifth, and sixth dynasty tombs ; that, marvellous as is the skill of the wall decorators in the spacious times of that great Elizabeth of old Egypt, Queen Hātshepset * of the seventeenth dynasty, 1600 B.C., as evidenced on the walls of her terraced temple of Deir El Bahari at Thebes, the hand of the sculptor and painter is quite as skilful in the times when Tih and Ptah-hotep entered their " houses of eternity," in the fifth dynasty, say more than 1800 years before that date, in 3400 B.C.

But the tombs of Tih and Ptah-hotep † are forgotten in the excellent beauty of sculpture and colour of the pre-pyramid days, and it is to the oldest necropolis of Egypt we must turn to find examples of that ancient art.

---

* Spelt also Hatasû.   † Spelt also Thi and Ptah-hetep.

CHAPTER II.

ONE has a general way of thinking and speaking as if
the Pyramid times were the oldest whereof Egypt has
record; and, standing at the top of Chufu's Pyramid,
and looking down over the long lines of mastăbas to
the west, one thinks that one is surely gazing on the
tomb chambers of the earliest men who hereabout
entered rest.

But one is rudely wakened from this dream. Away
to the north the round-headed bastion-hill of Abu
Roâsh reminds us that there, amid the tons of little
votive pots and platters that bestrew the ground, once
rose the temples and tomb-chambers of some king who
had entered his eternal house before the Pyramids of
Gîzeh were thought of; and, again, if one gazes to
the south, one sees the curious-shaped Step Pyramid
of six terraces, each terrace 30 to 38 feet in height
above the other, towering up from a base 352 by 396,
to a height of 197 feet. That is the Pyramid of

Kochome, or the Black Bull Place. That was the
tomb of a King Ata, or Uenephes, the fourth king of
the first dynasty, of whom tradition says that " in his
time there was sore famine in Egypt ; nevertheless, it
pleased him to employ his people in building of this
pyramid." Who knows, it may have been a bit of
work given to the people, that by it they might earn
bread. All that one need realise, as the western sun
turns the distant pyramid into steps of gleaming
amethyst, is, that there-under was laid to rest the
builder of the oldest monument in Egypt—nay, the
oldest existing tomb monument in the world.

But one wishes to hear and see something of the
life of that distant time, and King Ata and his Step
Pyramid in this matter are dumb.

It is not till one has left Kochome, the site of the
"Black Bull," and passed on along the Nile for another
twenty miles to the south, that one finds oneself
opposite another bull place, or Bull-town, Mi-Tum,
or Mêdûm, over which rises a gigantic tomb
monument, whose builder has left behind him actual
records of his life, and about whose mighty pyramid
lie tombs of princes and princesses that come forth
out of their dust and speak to us plainly of the days,
in the dawn of Egyptian history.

King Seneferu, last of the third dynasty, or first of
the fourth dynasty, may have had that older Step
Pyramid in his mind when he determined to build this

great blunt-topped pyramid, 115 feet high, in three
stages of 70, 20, 25 feet, of the white Mokattam limestone. And "He who makes Good"—for that is believed to be the strict meaning of the name " Seneferu "
—was determined to make good his mason-work. It
is in finish exquisite.

With Seneferu began the custom of adding to the
cartouche that bore the name his parents gave him, a
second cartouche containing his holy name ; and, in
addition to this, of adding to the double cartouche
three sounding titles : " The Sun Hor, who dispenses
light and life, blessing and prosperity ; " " The Lord of
both Kingly Diadems ; " " The Image of Honour of
the Golden Hor, the conqueror of his opponent." But
it is not only that he was " Maker of the Good," but
that he was styled " Lord of Truth," that makes this
kingly personage in the dawn of Egyptian history so
interesting.

Benevolence and justice were evidently felt to be
sovereign powers in pre-pyramid days, the days of
B.C. 3766, the days when Seneferu was king.

I said that Seneferu was the first king of ancient
Egypt who stands clearly out as a living ruler. Ata
may have built his Step Pyramid 500 years before his
time, but then, except as a name and a legend, Ata
has perished from among the children of men ; but
the traveller in the Sinaitic peninsula may see clearly
to-day, carved on the rocks above the " mafkat," or

" turquoise " mines in Wady Maghara, a picture in stone of this remarkable monarch Seneferu, " Vanquisher of Foreign Peoples," as he is styled, who worked the mines and smote with the sword the dwellers in the wild hills, whose children should one day try conclusions, in sight almost of those turquoise mines, with Moses, the Man of God, and his Hebrew horde.

Professor Rawlinson in his " Ancient Egypt," in the " Story of the Nations " Series, p. 3, c. 55, gives an excellent sketch of the King Seneferu as he is there figured, smiting down with his stone-headed club one of those Sinaitic foemen—a stone picture which I remember gazing upon with double interest, as it gave me an idea how, and with what arms, the kings of his day fought when they worked their mafkat mines, and drilled the rock in quest of turquoises.

Seneferu, " the Maker of the Good," Seneferu, " the Lord of Truth," Seneferu, the mining engineer, Seneferu, " the Vanquisher of Foreign Peoples ; " Seneferu, of whom it was written in the old Theban historical papyrus, " Then was raised up the holiness of King Seneferu as a good king over the whole country," was determined to live again in the eyes of far-off centuries, and the rock-picture of Wady Maghara gives us a very lively image of the masterful king.

But Seneferu believed also that his body should rise again ; and so, in a lonely place to the far south, when as yet only two pyramids—the pyramid of Abu Roâsh, to the far north, and the Step Pyramid of Ata, fourth king of the first dynasty—lifted up their shining masses from the Libyan desert sands, Seneferu planned a mighty pyramid which he called the " Pyramid of the Rising," or Resurrection, and added a third great monument of gleaming masonry that should eclipse the tombs of all who went before or after, and keep his body safe, and his name secure, through all ages.

The Nile traveller, if he has a heart, will probably at the end of his voyage find the words " Mi Tum," or Bull Town, written upon it, for that glorious Mê- dûm pyramid, with its three stages of shining masonry lifting themselves to heaven, out of the brown mound of *débris* at its base, haunts the mind; and after many days the traveller finds that none of the temples and tombs he has seen up Nile, has banished the impression made by that lonely pile, whose triple-terraced, mountainous mass of yellow stone rises from the border of the plain of farmers' paradise, to the west of Wasta, fifty-five miles south of Cairo.

Whose tomb was it? That was not exactly known till quite recently. It had been said to have been built by King Seneferu, the founder of the fourth Egyptian dynasty, about 3766 B.C., but savants had cast doubts upon this, and it has been left for Mr. Flinders Petrie to show, by patient excavation, that, at any rate as long ago as the time of Amenophis III., and Thothmes I., and Seti I., the pyramid in question was looked upon as Seneferu's building—Seneferu, " Lord of Truth " and " Maker of the Good," who was long after his death looked upon as a god— Seneferu, whose temple, perhaps owing to this fact, still stands intact at the base of his vast pyramid tomb to this day.*

One had often heard of the False Pyramid, as the Fellaheen call it, Haram el-Kaddab—calling it so, because, in their ignorance of the plan of pyramid building, they thought that these steps, which their fathers had made to appear, by a process of stripping the pyramid of outer casing, were evidence that the pyramid had never been finished. One had thought of it as being, for all this " falseness " or unfinished- ness of appearance, the oldest pyramid — Sakkara's Step Pyramid only excepted — standing in Egypt. One had fancied the men hard at work piling stone, down at Mêdûm, before ever the quarrymen had been called upon to hew a block in the quarries of Mokattam and Turra at the command of Chufu, Chafra, or Menkaura. And so one had much wished to see this forerunner of the pyramids at Gîzeh.

Even if the pyramid of Seneferu should, on nearer

* Seneferu is said by Brugsch Bey to have been the last king of the third dynasty, date 3766 ; by Mariette Bey, who dates the third dynasty as commencing B.C. 4449, he is looked upon as first king of the fourth dynasty, date B.C. 4235.

acquaintance, disappoint one with the manner of its masonry, or the finish of it, at any rate close by were mastăbas of the fourth dynasty; there were the tombs of Nefer Mât and Atot his wife, with their almost unique evidence of early Egyptian mosaics, by way of ornament, and then, side by side with these, there would be visible, we hoped, the tomb-chamber in which Mariette found those two remarkable life-size sitting statues in stone, of Rahotep and his wife Nefert, whose liquid eyes and delicate drapery and colouring are the marvel of the Gîzeh Museum.

So it needed little persuasion on the part of the great gloriously shining Pyramid of Mêdûm to call one from the Nile steamer, and bid one make one's way across the plain to its base.

We had hoped to accomplish our visit between sunrise and 3 P.M., when we knew the solitary afternoon train would have conveyed us from Rekkah, up through the evening lights of the rich Nile land to Cairo, but our steamer stuck, now here, now there, and it was already half-past four when we stopped the engines off the mud village of Rekkah, or Riggah, and with a bundle of food in our hands and a sailor to carry a donkey-saddle, we bade adieu to our fellow-passengers and pushed off for the Nile bank.

It is not so easy a matter as at first might appear, this landing from a Nile boat on a Nile bank, for the Nile mud is as slippery as grease, and what looks solid is found to be soft, and *vice versâ*. But we did not mind getting in up to the knees for the sake of good King Seneferu; and, struggling from the slime, we got on to the hot sand, and entering the dirty little village, asked for the railway station. We did not want a train, but we wanted donkeys, and we believed that the station-master, who in these out-of-the-way villages is the centre of light and learning, would be the provider of so much ass-flesh as would bear us to the pyramid. He could talk English a little, we spoke Arabic a little, and at once he despatched a bare-legged railway porter in blue blouse and red tarboosh to harry Rekkah for donkeys. "One donkey he knew of; Allah might give two, but of this he was not sure." Heaven smiled upon us, for a shout was heard half a mile away, and that shout echoed another half mile; there was a running together of camels and buffaloes and sheep in a very far-off field, and a little cloud of dust upon the railway-line embankment told us that our ass had been caught and was coming down the six-foot, at its own pace, to bear the "Khawaja" to Mêdûm.

We saddled up, and the donkey's master tapping the patient creature on the nose, for bridles are an unknown quantity in the Mêdûm donkey-world, we went back up the highway—the railway-line, for a quarter of a mile. We then turned into the pleasant green fields of beans and clover, and while the larks sang, and the paddy-birds strutted, and the kites flew high, we passed towards the sunset and the mighty memorial tomb of Seneferu.

Away to our right, as we rode over the rich plain towards the barren desert mounds, was seen the little palm-girt village of Ghurzeh; on our left, to the south, like barren islands in a sea of greenery, appeared the villages of Soft, Kafr Soft, and Haram or Haram Soft; whilst between Kafr Soft and Haram Soft was visible the tiny village that was the centre of the great religious world of the fourth dynasty in this place— the Bull Town, " Mi Tum "—Mêdûm of to-day.

It was good to hear how the old names had clung to these villages. No one would have thought, from looking upon that little village nearest the desert, by which our path presently took us, that there had once stood close by a pyramid; but as late as thirty years ago, the remains of a pyramid were visible there, and the present village is built out of the mud bricks that the old pyramid-builders made.

We wind in and out, now west, now south, for the lands are divided out in squares, and we go along the edges of the allotments. Whole families are squatting by their yellow-faced, lop-eared sheep, or their long-eared goats or grunting buffaloes. Here a tiny tot of a child watches a tethered camel, there a little girl carefully collects into a palm basket the manurial products of the day of cattle-feeding, to take home with her flock in the evening. A slinger crouches like a black ghoul—for he has drawn the head-shawl over his head—upon his rough clod hillock, and in the fields men are busy with hoe or glebe-hatchet and creaky "shadoofs." The land of Seneferu has no rest, and since the King of Truth and Goodness entered his tomb until this day, men plough and break the glebe and lift the shadoof bucket, and sling the stone, and take at morn the cattle to the fields, watch them through the day with greater care than they give to their children, and bring them back at eventide.

Now, while the hoopoe calls "hut-hut" from the distance, and the black and white kingfisher—"sick-sak"—poises over the village pond, we pass the remains of some old offering-stool or slab used in a temple, raised by the fourth dynasty men, but now cast out by the wayside. Round the muddy pond we go, wherein the ducks dabble and the brickmaker dabbles too, treading the slime into paste, filled full with the bits of chopped straw that have sunk down from farm-yard refuse of last year. This is the village of the pyramid we spoke of, and brickmakers, having exhausted the fourth-dynasty supply, must tread their own mud into brickage, and put it in their little square wood moulds and leave it to the sun.

We have now reached the edge of the plain, yellow here from the flower of the "kabbach" or ketlock, and here is a white-domed shêkh's tomb beside a fine old "atli," or juniper tree : beneath it rest the bones of Shêkh Ali Nurr—peace to his ashes. On now over the waste we go southward towards the shining terraced pyramid.

Presently we are aware that the great brown grey mounds upon our right and left have been trenched through, pits or wells are opened out in the midst, and what seemed just wind-blown waves of desert sand, show themselves to be carefully built mud-brick masses. We are in the burying-ground of oldest Egypt, and these are the mastăbas that extend from here to the foot of the pyramid, and on beyond it, which day by day, under the careful exploration of Mr. Flinders Petrie, are yielding up their secrets. Now we see a tiny tent and rough reed hut, such as the wandering Bedouin might use. This is the palatial accommodation that the brave explorer is contented with. If you go into that tiny tent, you will find an old packing-case with three rough shelves in it, a couple of cups, a plate, a spoon, a paraffin stove, a box of biscuits and some potted-meat tins ; and opposite, another packing-case to serve as table and chair in one. That is Mr. Petrie's dining and drawing room. If you enter the little tomb close by, where once, with much lamentation and many cakes of offering, entered those who mourned for Nefer Mât, you will see a rude camp bedstead. There, at the end of long days of digging, sleeps the explorer, and the stars can look in upon him, and the first sun visit him.

I brought no cakes of offering to the tomb; half a fowl and a bit of bread and a couple of oranges were my supply, but I found it all too much; for my friend the explorer opened his tin, and set his lamp a-going, and gave me of his store a supper fit for Seneferu; lent me his own pocket-knife to eat my feast, shared his single teaspoon with me, and finished piling on his desert courtesy with a bit of crystallised ginger, such as Seneferu and Nefer Mât never knew. I proffered my English bread in return; he haughtily refused it. What was English bread to a man who can get the Arab bread thrice a week from Wasta? I suggested that fowl recently killed and cooked would be a pleasant addition to his supper. He fiercely refused to believe me: had he not potted pilchards in abundance, and did not Moir supply him with English or Australian lambs' tongues in tins, that were better than all the fowls of the Nile valley? But I anticipate.

It was enough for me to know that that tiny tent and hut of reeds and tomb-chamber was the home of the "Khawaja," and to my question, "Where was he?" I was told " Gedam foh fil Haram," which, being interpreted, meant, " On there beyond, near the pyramid."

I went across the heaving billows of sand and flint, and found him taking some trigonometrical measures, which needed that he should not be interrupted till the sunlight failed him, and climbing up over the *débris* at the base of the pyramid, I wondered at its mass and its marvellous colour.

The hawks, beloved of Seneferu, Rahotep, and Nefer Mât in the days of auld lang syne, flew out and in to their high-built eyries, and clamoured as they flew. I looked up the eastern face of the masonry, and noted that, for a third of its height, it had upon it a rough facing of stone, then came tooled and smoothed orange-coloured limestone, and then a small band of rough-hewn stone. The meaning of this rough masonry, Mr. Petrie showed me after, was that two outer skins of casing, now destroyed, went upwards, the one to the top of the rough masonry, the other to the top of the second band. What labour had been lost here! All that careful tooling of the intermediate band of gloriously golden masonry had been covered over by one of those outer casings. All honour to the men for this waste of time, who, pending the putting on of the skin, dared to face this wall so beautifully with their facing tools.

At my feet, as I stood, I noticed the solid platform blocks of limestone masonry, all with a slight inward cant, whereon one of these outer skins had been built. Going a little farther to the north side, one could note the platform *in situ* wherefrom had sprung the second outer casing, and at the opening of the pyramid vault, which was discovered by Mariette Bey, the great trench his workmen made in the *débris* beneath was

still to be seen. One observed, as one bent forward
into the opening, and placed one's eyes against the
lintel and gazed upward, how, contrary to expectation,
these two outermost casings would run at an angle of
75 degrees clear to the top, beyond and outside of
the present terrace of masonry above, and give to the
six-stepped pyramid its possibility of pure pyramidal
form.

I do not think I could ever have realised how these
pyramid-builders built core within core, and, filling
up the terrace angles, got complete pyramid form,
had I not stood upon the outer casings of this pyramid
of Seneferu. I am sure I could not have got an idea of
the actual mass of building required, had I not
realised on the spot that all that vast mound, wherefrom the three or four central cores of the pyramid
that still remain intact arise, was nothing in the world
but the remnants of the two outer skins and the
débris occasioned by the stripping off of the upper
portions of these skins, and learned that it was con-
jectured that within the last three generations no less
than 100,000 tons of material had been carted away,
and that still the work of destruction and carting
away goes on. No "raphir," or local guardian, has
been appointed. Is £12 a year too large a sum to
expect of the Museum authorities towards the care of
this interesting fourth-dynasty Necropolis? It looks
like it.

And now the great sun was collecting its fire into
its bosom, and lighting up the bastion wall of Seneferu
till it burnt pure gold. White as milk is the limestone which Seneferu's builders originally piled.
Yellow as orange is the limestone to-day that has
been visited by more than 5000 years of rolling
suns.

Looking upward to the vault of heaven, one noted
that the deep orange accentuated the blue of the airy
pavilion above, and I thought of Faber's lines, " On
the Larch in Autumn," whose tresses are much in
colour as this pyramid wall is to-day :

> There is no tree in all the forest thro'
> That brings the sky so near and makes it seem so blue.

At any rate, I never saw Egyptian sky so blue as
when I looked at sunset time up the golden wall of
Seneferu's pyramid.

It was plain that Mr. Petrie had been digging for
the peribolos wall, and had found trace of it on all
four sides of the pyramid base. Going round the
pyramid, on the *débris* of the outer casing, towards
the east, one turned one's back upon the billowy
purple desert, and faced as fine a view as can be
gained in Egypt, a view certainly unequalled as far as
a Nile valley scene goes, for, though the view from the
pyramid of Chufu at Gîzeh is wonderful, one is
always oppressed by the somewhat keen sense of the
neighbourhood of mighty companions. Here one

C

looked out from the waist-belt of a solitary giant of stone, and nothing dwarfed the details of the scene.

The green plain with purple streaks of yellow stretched boundlessly north and south, licked the desert to the west with its green tongue, flooded with tender flood of cornland, a kind of inland bay that the great god Nile had made to the north beyond the tomb of Shêkh Ali Nurr.

The hills Gebel es Sherki, the hills to the far east across the valley, were white and grey, and seemed lower than the hill-plateau of Mokattam and Turra; the Nile was unseen, but belts of palm told us where he hid his silver head. All along at the foot of the desert-plateau whereon Seneferu built his mighty tomb, ran the tiny strip of silver canal that gave water to the thirsty villagers and parching fields. By its banks were going homeward at the sunset, flocks and herds, the whole air was filled with the sound of labourers and laughing lads and lasses who were picking up heart, now that rest and food-time were so near ; and mason bees, who had plastered the whole side of the eastern face of the masonry above us, added their sound of pleasant murmuring.

The shadow of the pyramid, a cone-pointed sloping tower of blackness, moved and stretched itself upon the vivid green. There was no other shadow in that land. So full of peace and rest was the scene that

the men who had been long dead came out of their
tombs and mastăbas north and east, and I seemed to
see them passing up the hollow *dromos*, between the
white walls Mr. Petrie has uncovered, from the green
plain towards the peribolos wall, or passing in from
the north and south to the side entrance of that
avenue he has laid bare, and so up towards the little
temple of offerings for the manes of King Seneferu,
and for the rest in Amenti of the founder of the
fourth dynasty.

I was very anxious to be of their ghostly company,
so I went down the shales of limestone *débris* to
where the workmen still plied mattock and palm-
basket among the silver smoke of the rubbish they
were moving. For Mr. Petrie had determined to dig
a way through the rubbish to the eastern entrance
gate of the temple, and let as much light within the
temple chamber, as should serve for himself and his
photographic apparatus, to put on record the *graffiti*
of certain scribes who had passed into that chamber,
in the days when Thothmes III. and Amenophis III.
and Seti I. were kings.

Mr. Petrie had finished his labours for the day, and
joined me; and not without a proper enthusiasm and
a just pride did he show me his discovery of the
oldest piece of dated masonry in Egypt, the most
complete archaic temple in the land of Nile.

For here, untouched by the hand of the spoiler,

was a small temple completely roofed in, with little
forecourt, say roughly twelve feet square, reaching to
the base of the untouched outer casing of Seneferu's
pyramid.   On either side the doorway two milk-white
monoliths, chipped at the base, but *in situ* and otherwise intact, raised their shining height.   These stelæ
stood about eight feet high, and two and a half by one
foot broad, and between them lay a stone of offerings
on which men had poured oil and left the fruits of
the earth in memory of their king, "The Maker of
Good," who, ages after he was laid in his sarcophagus,
was looked upon as God.

I passed from the sanctuary into the chamber
through the low door, and can but describe it as a
long box, twenty feet long by about six or eight feet
broad, and five feet high, somewhat like the four
lateral chambers in the inner court of the granite
temple near the south-west side of the sphinx at Gîzeh.
The chamber was built of large blocks of limestone
carefully fitted, and showing in parts that it was still
in process of being dressed down, or tooled when the
craftsmen left it; it sparkled with diamonds of salt
that had worked their way out to the surface.   Passing thence by a low doorway at the north end, one
found a similar hollow box of limestone, laid parallel
with the first chamber, and at the farther or south
end, and on the east side, a passage leading eastward
—this, in fact, the main entrance passage, long blocked

up, which Mr. Petrie's workmen were still busied in
clearing.   And here, opposite this passage, and in
the passage itself, was centred the interest of the
find ; for about fourteen *graffiti*, some in the passage,
some on the western wall of the entrance chamber,
or so much of it as could be lighted from the entrance
passage, were seen as fresh as when penned.   In the
passage was one written by a scribe in the reign of
Thothmes III., 1600 B.C.   On the chamber wall were
others written when Amenophis III., 1500 B.C., and
Seti I., 1366 B.C., were on the throne.

One especially, of the latter was of interest, for
there was a long inscription of fourteen or sixteen
lines of close hieratics, whose date-sign had been
inscribed in red, and therein the word Seneferu occurred in three places, and so a vexed question was
settled.   This temple was reared before the pyramid
that in Seti I.'s time, at any rate, was looked upon as
the Pyramid of Seneferu.   Seneferu was the royal
genius of this place as long ago as 1366 years B.C.

Two little drawings, roughly scrawled, adorned the
wall, one of them a disk of the sun—looking, save
the mark, like a watch face—and beside it a seated
Osiris figure; the other picture was an image of
Horus as a hawk, whose legs were long enough to
have done duty for a heron—beneath it a *graffito* of
the time of Amenophis III.

It looked very much as if these scribbling scribes

came, as I had come, on errand of curiosity, and had not been able to penetrate to the second chamber, or to the sanctuary between the statues. There, perhaps, darkness reigned in their time, there *débris* had perhaps fallen, and, luckily for our century and our eyes, had covered in the shrine where men of Seneferu's day had worshipped with their faces toward the base of the sloping pyramid. Surely the narrow area of the inscriptions in the first chamber looks, as Mr. Petrie suggested, much as if at the doorway alone light could penetrate the first temple chamber, and thither only came the scrawlers of hieratics.

The light was fading fast, but Mr. Petrie showed me how he had first come upon the outer wall of the sanctuary by driving a trench through the *débris* from the south, and he also pointed out how, after the sanctuary had been almost cleared, a strong wind rose—I do not think the gods were angry—and cast down tons of the chip *débris* from above, and gave him all his work to be done again; but drawings have now been made.

For the sake of travellers, one could wish that a "raphir," or local guardian, could be appointed, at a pound a month, to see that this archaic temple was not injured, and that it was kept clean and clear of rubbish; yet I am not sure but that, perhaps, the sealing up of Mr. Petrie's important find, by the chip *débris* from above, will not be the safest way of pre-

serving that which it has so well preserved all down
the centuries until to-day. And here, above our
heads, as we talked, hung the chip-sealing; a single
gun-shot fired, and all would be reburied again!

Home we went to the tiny tent and the cup of tea
—never tea, though milk was not, tasted better—and
the stars were over us as we talked of the work done
during the last months in this ancient necropolis.

To the east of the pyramid Mr. Petrie had investi-
gated two mastăbas. The outer casing of both had
been unburnt Nile-mud bricks. I measured one, and
found it to be 14 × 7 × 6 inches—large bricks, well
kneaded with chopped straw, and tough even to-day.
The inside of one mastăba was completely filled with
chips from the *débris* of the pyramid builders; the
core of the other was filled with remnants of pottery
from the offerings that had come to the shrine of the
pyramid temple.

But other discoveries of interest had been made at
the former mastăba, for at the angles, Mr. Petrie had
laid bare angle-walls upon which the builders had
drawn, in black and red, the lines of inclination or
angle at which they intended the mastăba builders
to build their mastăba's slope. I had a good look
at these angle-walls early on the following morning,
and was surprised at the brilliancy of the colouring
of the broad, red, vertical line upon the white-cemented
angle-wall, and noted how accurate these old work-

men were even in the matter of line drawing. They had with a fine, red, double line first drawn their red vertical eye-guide, and had then filled in the middle space of it so as to preserve, in its absolute integrity and accuracy of outline, the standard upright for their line of sight. It was not without interest to note the horizontal cross-lines which had been drawn at intervals all the way up from the ground to the top of the angle-wall, at the distance of single cubit spaces apart, and that underneath, at one point, for the guidance of the foundation builders, had been written in red letters the note, " Under is the good, five cubits," which meant that the rock-bed was five cubits beneath this mark on the wall.

One sometimes talks of the want of care in foundations, that the old Nile valley builders were guilty of, but I confess that, after seeing this note, and observing the deep trench from which the outer lining mastăba wall sprang, and after looking carefully at the depth of masonry upon which the columns of Amenophis rest in the Temple of Luxor, one's idea of their want of knowledge of foundations has been considerably altered, and when one observes how cleverly the old architects used their red paint in the " construction " line, their black for the " working " line, so that the eye might never hesitate or become confused, one asks even if our own architects are wiser than the men of old !

That evening-talk in the tent was full of interest ; one learned much, but the best thing I learned was the kind of friendly relation existing between Mr. Petrie and his workmen. I had seen them labouring with their palm baskets and adze-shaped hoes till after sundown. Mr. Petrie had been late in taking observations, and so had not given his usual signal of a whistle for the men to cease work, but they did not cease, and I soon found that there had been established such relations between employed and employer as made the day's work not slaves' labour, but the work of men who wished to serve their master in love to the uttermost. There was a fair at some Fayûm village near, and some of the men came up to the tent very courteously to ask for their wages, and for leave to go. It was a sight worth seeing, the patient courtesy with which they squatted, one hand on the tent-pole, and listened to Mr. Petrie's recital of the various amounts due for the various metres' work on the different days. They kept nodding and saying " Aiwar" as the various details were given ; they were serving a just man, and they knew that each evening their work had been measured and recorded. Sometimes an extra piastre or two had been agreed upon for this or that extra work or extra care, and the men smiled and mentioned it, and took their wage, saying at what hour they intended to return, but all with such an air of confidence and pleasure in their talk as made one feel that the curse of Egypt had been lifted, and that labour and joy had supplanted the labour and curse of the old kourbash days.

" Well, you see," said my friend, " that I first carefully pick my men. I then get the fathers and the children to work together. Each hand is soon found to be better fitted for one kind of work than another, and I change the men's work till I find each man is in the right place, and then the work goes on smoothly. I have no ' reis,' or intermediate man ; I go round each day to see the men at their various posts, and instead of massing them together at one big job, in which they would only get in one another's way, I tell them off to the different points of exploration, and agree to pay by the metre, and thus discount idleness." I went back in thought to that very different method of excavation I had seen at Luxor and Karnak, and wished devoutly the Gîzeh Museum authorities would take a leaf out of Mr. Petrie's book. Here, at the Mê-dûm, men and master were, it seemed, bound by a common tie of interest, which seemed of a really personal character. There, at Luxor and Karnak, a great cursing and swearing bully in the form of a "reis," armed with a kourbash, hustled the children with their palm baskets of mould, from pit to bank, lashing them mercilessly at times, and flicking his elephant-hide whip, as it would seem for pure cruelty's sake, at the thinly clad or half-naked bodies of the

poor little girls and boys who were, in the name of
Science working like slaves through heat and dust, to
bring back the colossi of Rameses the Great, or the
temple of his father Seti, from the grave of centuries.

It was a sight to make any Englishman's heart boil
to see the lash, in the hand of the burly bully at the
pylon of Luxor, curl with a crack round the leg of a
lad or naked ankle of a girl, with a heavy palm basket
on their heads, as they toiled up the steep bank, and
bring the poor creatures to their knees ; but when I
complained I was told " Ma-alesh" (" It matters not ");
" Mafish kourbash, shoggalu mafish " (" No kourbash,
no work "). I have seen the men and boys who are
working pleasantly and cheerfully for Mr. Petrie at
Mêdûm, and I unhesitatingly say that he gets twice as
much of actual work done in the time, as the brute who
drives his gang of slaves at Luxor and Karnak ; and I
know, from seeing them labour at early morn and to late
eventide, with what interest and pleasure—I was going
to say with what pride—they work for " Khawaja
Engleese," the English gentleman. It was refreshing
to sit there in the shadow of those vast mastăba
mounds, at the building of which we had been
brought up to believe the land had groaned, and
the lash had been lifted, and the sweat of the people
toiling for its princes had been taken for nought, and
to see how now, men laboured with the same tools,
dressed in the same way, having much the same

simple wants to satisfy, and the same homes to come from and return to at morn and eventide—but a light was in their faces and a smile upon their lips, for they toiled for honest bread at honest price, and their master was a friend.

I say this because that evening I heard a boy's voice and saw a boy's hand thrust through the tent, and noticed Mr. Petrie solemnly cut a bit of soap in two and give the lad half, saying, "I find there's nothing like soap for sore heads." Presently another voice piped in the darkness, and the same knife now dived into a pot of ointment, and spread some carefully on a sore place near the nose of the applicant— a dust sore, for which this ointment was a palliative.

Presently, with a low salaam, a dusky man, with a dark ache in his dusky stomach, applied for cure. The paraffin lamp was kindled. A cup of coffee was made, and therein a spoonful of pepper stirred. The poor fellow swallowed it with a gurgle, and turned to go. "God increase your goods exceedingly!" ("Ya Kattar Allah kherak. Katall kherak ketîr!") was the word of thanks; and the grateful ones went back to their reed huts and their burnouses and their sandy beds for the night.

I did not wonder that Mr. Petrie, the wise hâkîm, was beloved of his workmen. Fancy a poor sick or wounded child coming to the Luxor bully with the kourbash, for emollient or detergent! What a change had come over the labourers' dream here under the shadow of the Mêdûm Pyramid! And what a different estimate of the qualities and character of the Egyptian Fellah was this that we gained by converse with the explorer, from the ordinary guide-book idea that prevails with Nile travellers! A letter received afterwards from Mr. Petrie is so confirmatory of what we saw and felt, that I dare to print it.*

---

* "With regard to the treatment of workers, you may say that I have never found occasion to strike a man or child that was in my pay, during ten years' work. This is not from any sentimental reason (for I heartily believe in the *kurbash* as a penal measure), but simply that no one is worth employing who needs punishing. My only penalty is inexorable dismissal, without warning. Sometimes I take a fellow back, where it was only a squabble between workers; but *never* if asked to do so.

"For three years now I have had no overseer or headman; there is no one between me and the workers; and I much prefer it. All overseers expect to get a heavy proportion of the wages, and *do* get it. I believe that of every £1000 spent on works, from £200 to £300 goes into the pockets of men who have not the faintest right to it. When the railway was lately made in the Fayûm the wages were enough, but the exactions of the 'reises' were such that few men cared to take the work for what *they* got. Hence it dragged on a long time for lack of enough labour. Probably the engineers had no idea of the cause.

"My workmen always form my natural guards and friends, and I have never known them steal anything. On the contrary, they will often dispute an account against their own interest, and if accidentally paid too much in error, they will bring me back the money and go over it. Even when any visitor gives a boy

Next morning we were awake with the lark; the great sun drove his fleecy flocks from the plains of the Nile to the plains of heaven, and the green carpet of the valley was already alive with the shouts " of labourers going forth into the fields " below us as we gazed.

We paid a second visit to the pyramid and the archaic temple, towards which we saw the workmen coming from the near village, and streaming up the slope of *débris* to their toil, palm-baskets and hoe over their shoulders. One man had broken his basket handle, and I noticed with interest his fellow-labourer produce from his bosom a bit of palm fibre in the

---

a piastre or two for any little service, they will generally come and tell me, as a piece of news that they like to share with me. I mention this to show you what terms I am on with them. Yet I get work done cheaper than any one else does, at two-thirds of the lowest rate of Government contract. So it is not merely extravagant pay that they look after. I have an excellent opinion of the Egyptian when under authority; but he cannot stand temptation, especially long-continued; hence it is criminally wrong to throw temptations in their way, and I am very careful to avoid doing so.

"I always pay the men for whatever they find, just what I expect they would get from a travelling dealer. So they have no temptation to conceal anything.

" If you can do anything toward abolishing this horrible, effete system of leaving all the management in the hands of corrupt and overbearing ' reises,' it will be a good work. I believe that very few natives are fit to exercise authority."

rough, and in less time than it takes me to write, sit down and twist it into rope, rolling it like tobacco twist between his clever hands into four-stranded cord.

Thence we went to see the pits to the north side of the mastăbas, where the angle-walls before described had been uncovered. These had contained burials of the twenty-second dynasty, which varied in depth from 6 to 30 feet. It looked as if whole families had selected the mud walls and inner lining of the mastăba as a kind of quarry wherein they could with ease excavate the narrow cells for their long sleeping. The place was many-caverned, and looked, after Mr. Petrie's work, like a warren of some gigantic earth-burrower. Here a whole family had been content to burrow little cells, 12 feet deep, side by side; there, and apparently in some long anterior age that the later buriers knew nothing of, men had sunk their deep wells and lowered the heavy stones to close the side chamber, at the bottom of the well.

Although, as at Kom es Sultân, so here, it seemed the deeper he dug, the older were the burials, not one of the least remarkable discoveries Mr. Petrie had made was this, that side by side with one another, and apparently buried at the same age, there appeared to be two different races of men, or at any rate men with two different ideas about burial. In one grave will be found men laid out full length; in another,

with equal care, the bodies of men have been doubled
up in a crouching position, knees to chin ; but these
last have always most carefully been laid upon their
left side, their heads to the north and their faces to
the east. As to the men laid out full length, these
were placed sometimes in rude coffins of wood, fragments of which remained ; the coffins had been
covered with stucco. One mummy had been found
modelled as it were in pitch—the pitch, that is, not
poured over and left in a formless mass, but carefully
worked so as to cover the limbs in normal human
proportion. No implement, so far as I learnt, had
been discovered in any of the graves, and such fragments of pottery as appeared, resembled the rough
little offering-vases one finds in such numbers at Abu
Roâsh. I think the Abu Roâsh pots are, if anything,
a trifle rougher in make, but they are of similar shape
to the tiny third- or fourth-dynasty vases discovered
by Mr. Petrie at the Mêdûm.

I crossed to examine the mastăbas and tombs to
the north-west, and stopped, of course, before the
door of Nefer Mât's tomb, a tomb which, since the
explorer took up his quarters here, might be spoken
of as

> A tomb contrived a double debt to pay—
> A bed by night, a drawing-room by day ;

for here Mr. Petrie was able, in the little guest-
chamber that Nefer Mât planned for the mourning of

his friends and relatives, to finish the plans, and put the colours to the beautiful drawings he has made, of the sculpture of the adjacent tombs.

The first thing that struck one was that the mastăba Nefer Mât had reared for his memorial, and for the well-chamber wherein his body rested, had apparently been finished, decorated with false doorways, and coated with limewash or cement, just as the inner wall of that ancient Egyptian fortress near Abydos had been coated, and that then an outside or masking wall had been built, entirely to cover the original mastăba. The limestone tomb-chamber seemed to have been excavated in the original mastăba, and the outer lining or casing may perhaps have entirely covered and concealed the entrance to the tomb-chamber at some later time. Be that as it may, I was face to face with the open tomb-chamber of a nobleman, who was probably of the household of the king who built what Mariette Bey called " the most carefully constructed and best built pyramid in Egypt," and I naturally expected to find that he carried on the traditions of the great Seneferu, and Erpah Nefer Mât did not disappoint one. For here upon the outer wall, at the left hand of the doorway, the resolute-looking man stood—square-headed, features delicate, small beard, his hair curled after the manner of the day—unless it was a short-frizzed wig he wore; and, not content with the beautiful sculpturing

D

in low relief, so characteristic of that dawn of Egyptian art history, this man, who lived before the Gîzeh pyramids, had determined to have his image on his doorway of brilliant mosaic, and there are the pit marks in the stone for the colour to this day, some of them still holding the red cement or enamel which was used for the decoration of his waist-cloth 3750 years B.C.

I had, under Mr. Grébaut's guidance, seen on a low wall flanking the western side of the inner part of Amenophis' hall of columns at Luxor, rude pit marks in the stone, which had doubtless been filled once with a like enamel, but then there, the pit marking was rougher, and this enamelling that I was gazing at, was more than 2000 years earlier in date. But it was not only the manner of enamelling that interested one in Nefer Mât's tomb : the beauty of the stone sculpture was, for clear cutting, wonderful. Nefer Mât had been father of three sons : there they were upon the left-hand door soffit—the eldest a man, the youngest a child. He had had a beloved wife, the Lady Atot : she is sculptured on the wall to the right. He had been a great farmer, and each farm, mindful of the dead master, had sent a servant with offerings to his tomb; amongst them was seen the name of Mitum, the Bull-town, so that one could turn one's head and gaze upon the very fields that knew the lordship of Nefer Mât in the time of the third or fourth dynasty, for there, in the plain below, was to be seen the brown-mud cluster of huts upon its mound, that still kept its village name of Bull-town, or Mêdûm.

And Nefer Mât had been a lover of sport in the days of long ago, for here, unhooded, on their several perches, immediately above the doorway, sat, as they had sat in stone miniature for more than 5500 years, the four favourite hawks of Erpah Nefer Mât.* He had died, one might suppose—or at any rate had prepared his tomb with thoughts of death before him —while still in the full vigour of his active out-door life ; and he had had a wife who must have shared his love of field sports, for on the façade of the Lady Atot's tomb, about 50 feet to the north, men are represented as spreading a large net for wild fowl, while three persons (perhaps the three sons who are sculptured on Nefer Mât's tomb) bring the fowl they have captured to the great hunter's dame, and the inscription tells us that " Princess Atot receives with pleasure the game caught alive by the chief noble Nefer Mât."

I noted also on the façade of the tomb the " khent "

* Mr. Harting, the secretary of the Linnæan Society, the author of a book that gives the bibliography and history of Falconry, has written me, saying that if the hawks so delineated are hunting hawks, then this inscription puts back the date of falconry, and makes it an old-world sport beyond what could have been imagined.

or quadruple libation-vase which was used in Nefer Mât's time to prevent jealousy among the gods, when oil was outpoured to the great god and the local triad, or to God under four aspects. "None were before or after other" in their various manifestations of deity, in the minds of worshippers, when men poured libations in the days of Atot and Nefer Mât.

I did not see the Lady Atot's tomb-chamber; the Arabs had so ruthlessly cut it about that Mr. Petrie had very properly filled it with sand; but I gazed reverently in the Gîzeh Museum at the marvellous fresco of geese that Mariette brought from the interior of Lady Atot's tomb-chamber, with the kind of wonder that one gazes at the earliest picture of the kind in the world; and as I gazed I felt that Lady Atot must not only have been as great a lover of the fowls of the farm as she was, with her husband, a lover of field-sport, but that she must have had an eye for natural history that would not allow of the drawing and colouring of a single false feather, by the artist she employed for her tomb-chamber's decoration.

Her artist, was for all purposes of finish, a Japanese. I turned to leave Nefer Mât's tomb, but not without a wonder at the way in which the great man had determined to tell after-ages that, in the time when Seneferu was king, men could handle stone in a way that would severely tax all our mechanical appliances of to-day. He had chosen that his tomb-chamber should be roofed with large slabs of limestone. The one exposed to view measured roughly 20 feet in length, 8 feet in breadth, and was 3 feet thick, and weighed probably 42 tons. But what was a weight of 42 tons for a roofing-stone in the days of the third dynasty?

We went up over the back of the mastăba, and visited two mastăba pits that Mr. Petrie had uncovered, thence to a mastăba farther to the north, and intermediate between the mastăba of Nefer Mât and Ra Hotep of Gîzeh Museum fame. Every one who visited Bulâk, or who now visits Gîzeh Museum, will remember those two almost life-size seated statues of limestone, spoken of as the oldest portrait-statues in stone that exist in Egypt, or, for the matter of that, in the world.

Ra Hotep, with his right hand on his breast, his left hand on his knee, sits naked, but for his waist-cloth, bareheaded, brown of skin, with a single jewel round his neck, side by side with his wife, the royal Lady Nefert. She, fair of skin and delicately clad in fine white linen garment, sits with folded arms—upon her head a dainty circlet of riband, a necklace of eight bands, the lower one with large pear-shaped stones, her hair frizzed into a fine wig, and her feet bare. No one who has once seen Ra Hotep and his wife Nefert forgets the liquid, limpid, life-like eyes—eyes of quartz and rock crystal upon a background of silver plate to give light ; and here I stood at the pit mouth, 30 feet in depth, down which had been lowered to their rest in the brown mud-brick mastăba, the bodies of Ra Hotep—son of Seneferu, as some say, " commander of the king's warriors, chief of the priests in the temple city of On, Heliopolis, the town of the god Ra "—and his princess-wife Nefert, " the beautiful," the king's granddaughter.

The great stone that sealed the tomb had been let down into its place by means of ropes, coiled eighty times round its massy bulk.   The rope had perished, but the impression of the twisted palm-fibre strands was still fresh when Mr. Petrie opened the pit.   No mummy of Ra Hotep was found, but men of Mr. Petrie's stamp are discouraged by nothing, not even when, as in the case of the neighbouring mastăba-well of Ra Nefer, he finds that others have burglariously entered the tomb from below, and long ago burrowed upward into the chamber, he with such arduous work has just worked his way down to.   But it is not only by burglars of old time that the explorer in Seneferu's necropolis to-day may be baffled, for sometimes such an untoward event happens as occurred in the opening of a mastăba pit, rather farther to the north than the one of Ra Hotep.   There, just as the workmen had finished clearing out a tomb-well, and were ready to descend to the tomb-chamber, a large black snake was seen to glide from the light

and disappear into the darkness ; and, of course, till
that snake was scotched and killed—a matter of no
little difficulty—no one would venture down to prose-
cute the work of inquiry.

But returning from the top of the mastăba, one
naturally wished to see the tomb-chamber, or shrine
itself, from which in January of 1872 Mariette Bey
removed the two oldest portrait statues in the world
to which a date can be assigned. And, thanks to
Mr. Petrie's work, one could see that a little forecourt,
with long low wing walls and two white limestone
pillars or stelæ, stood before the entrance to the
chamber; passing through this little forecourt, and
entering the painted and sculptured room, one noted
at once the comparative freshness of the colours, and
the hieroglyphs that stood out in exquisite relief : such
hieroglyphs, so cleanly carved, I have nowhere seen in
Egypt.

The little room, or ante-room, that we entered,
spread itself out into two wings, right and left, and
between these was a recess or shrine. The figures in
the Gîzeh Museum originally stood in front of this
recess. Ra Hotep is sculptured on the left wall, with
his long staff in hand, his three sons beside him.
His foot is firmly set down, and one observed an
exquisite bit of sculptor's accuracy in the way in
which the fold or crinkle of the flesh, between the
instep and the big toe, was expressed.

The Lady Nefert is seen, long-haired, with a lily in the fillet, and she holds one in her hand also; but I forgot all about Ra Hotep and his Lady Nefert in the children whose pictures and names were given on the jambs of the little innermost recess: Jeddah, Atori, and Nefer Ra, the brothers; and Neferab, Settet, and Mest, the sisters.

How delightful it was to think of that happy family life of old, when the father who called one daughter to his side always spoke of her as "Sweetheart," and Sweetheart, if she talked with her sister, always named her "The Beloved One."

In the upper registers of the side wings were seen sculptured the oryx, oxen, ibex; and in the four lower registers of the right-hand wing, Ra Hotep's seal-bearer, butcher, cup-bearer, and five servants bringing offerings were portrayed. The vases of honey were covered with lids and sealed down tightly, and beautiful in shape were the jars seen to be—one as delicate as a Greek vase, another evidently hewn out of stone. I suppose they worked with diamond drills, and cut the diorite with corundum into whatever shape it pleased them, when Seneferu was king, and Ra Hotep stood as a prince among the people.

In the opposite or left-hand wing of the chamber, representatives from twelve farms, men and women, brought offerings; and that Ra Hotep encouraged handicrafts, and cared for the life of the country

gentleman, was evident from the fact that here, in his
tomb-chamber, were seen men working with adze and
wedges shaping out wood, boat-builders were busy,
fishermen fished with nets that had floats and sinkers,
and a couple of men staggered under the weight of a
fish just caught, as big as a John Doree : ploughing
was going forward, herdsmen drove the calf afield, and
a man was seen coaxing a bull along.

But it was the bird-life of Ra Hotep's time that
charmed me.   The great man's three hawks were there,
but these were of small account when compared with
the interest of the wagtails drawn to the life.   For the
wagtail befriends every Nile traveller to-day, lights on
the deck of his dahabieh, comes into his cabin, and
as they are in colour and dress to-day, so I gather
from Ra Hotep's tomb they were in the days of
Seneferu ; they have not changed a single feather of
their dress, and they are the beloved bird of the family
of those who dwell beside the Nile to-day, as they were
then.   It is a long time that separates us from that
date.   The pyramids of Gîzeh had not been built
when these wagtails were sculptured and painted.
Men used stone knives and horn-stone hatchets then
—witness the sculptures on the walls ; and yet, as the
little figure of the fluted Doric pillars tells me, there,
on the tomb-chamber wall, at that time of day, they
hewed out pillars that were the forefathers of the glory
of the Parthenon, and knew how to work in high relief

their mural sculptures and hieroglyphics in style, scarcely surpassed when Hātshepset was queen; while as to pigment, here was colour, if anywhere, that had stood the test of time.

Yes, and it has had to stand crueller tests of late years. For an English "khawaja" opened this tomb-chamber for his pleasure some five years ago, and heartlessly left it open. He had his look, he was satisfied, and cared not one jot or tittle what should happen to this, the most remarkable monument of the third or fourth dynasty handicraft, in the necropolis of Mêdûm. He did not even let the Egyptian authorities know of his visit, or it is possible that the Museum directors would have at once prevented harm by filling the chamber, as Mariette had filled it, with the conserving sand. He came, he saw, he went away; and after him came Arabs, who saw, but did not go away, and the result is that [the splendour of Ra Hotep's tomb-chamber is a thing of the past; and as I left the great brown mastăba heaps, and, turning my back upon the glorious Pyramid of Seneferu, passed away, among the green corn and blossoming beanfields, towards the Nile, I did not think kindly of that English "khawaja," and thanked Heaven that the exploration of the necropolis of Seneferu was in such tender, careful hands as those of the patient worker, it had been my very good luck to find at work therein.

CHAPTER III.

HOW I SAW THE GREAT PHARAOH IN THE FLESH.
A REMINISCENCE OF THE BÛLÂK MUSEUM.

" COMING ? coming ? " shouted the blue-bloused, bare-legged donkey-boys. " No," I answered, " I am going. Fayn Khawaja ? "—" Where to ? " they shrieked. " Lel antîkât " (" To the House of Antiquities "), I replied. All the donkeys near seemed to have caught the last word, and, moved from an apparent within, which was found to be a most cruel without, twenty of them at least, with their humped saddles and gay saddle-cloths, were in a moment competing for the honour of carry-ing the English stranger to the Bûlâk Museum.

There was great consternation at finding that the English stranger talked broken Arabic, still greater when it was found he examined every donkey for the "raw," and refused the whole twenty rather than en-courage donkey-boy brutality. How I wish all travellers in Egypt would do the same. So off I trudged out of the Esbekîyeh, and so on through the acacia-shadowed avenue, past the residence of Stephenson, the English general in command, away towards that home of mercy and life, the German Deaconesses' Hospital, well pleased with the quiet and absence of donkey-boy scream and wheeze and sigh as they cry " Hah ! hah ! " with long-drawn gasps, behind their scampering donkeys. De-lighting in the red of the butterfly-like poinsettia, the purple of the bougainvillia, the dancing, glancing light and shadow of the acacias and lebbek trees, I was just congratulating myself upon the quietude, and watching a black Nubian take a whiff at the public pipe, which was kept lit by a bundle of rags that turned out to be a seller of coffee at the corner ; was just chuckling at the grotesqueness of another man, who, squat on the pavement, had had half of his ugly head shaved clean, and was looking at himself and his lathery other half of a skull in a bit of broken mirror, the street barber was holding up to him, when shouts of " Lel antîkât " filled the air, and it looked as if every donkey in Cairo donkeydom was rushing up, to secure the silver coin (about $3\frac{1}{2}d.$ in value) that would be gained by carrying me, the English stranger, across the mounds of rubbish, along by the Roman Catholic church, over or along the railway line, and on to the bridge across the canal, down by the barracks of Kasr-el-Nil, and so, for half a mile through old Bûlâk, to the famous museum by the riverside. One after another the donkey-boys lifted up their charges' tail-harness, to prove that their beasts were unwounded, and you would have laughed your heart out to see how, instead of the head, the tails of these wonderful creatures were all that were offered me; but I chose one, and crying, "Lel antikât, Muhhâmmad," away we went scampering over the rubbish heaps, while the kites flew like burnished bronze between me and the sun—away for a mile and a half towards the last resting-place of the mighty dead, whose favourite symbol of victorious life, in their worship, had been these hawks of the sun, these kites who circle, true conquerors of death, above the carrion of the city outskirts of to-day.

As I passed over the bridge by the barracks, I saw the kind of sight that Moses doubtless looked upon, before he smote the Egyptian and buried him in the sand. Here was Egypt in bondage, as Israel of old had been. Three hundred ragged men in skull-caps, bare many of them to the waist, were ranged in files, as close as could be, from the canal bottom to the top of the steep banks, handing up great cakes of mud and clay, and the filth of a city canal-bottom, and so deepening the canal and heightening its banks—dredging by hand with a vengeance, whilst the officer in command shouted and yelled, and used his stick as only a Cairene Jack-in-office can do.

As we cantered through the busy street of Bûlâk on each side were the little shops, while on a wooden platform sat the vendor, his whole shop, front and back, filled with corn and fruits of Egypt. Here were the brownish-red bean, the golden-yellow lentils, the grey peas, the white barley, the gold-red wheat. Camels laden with green " bersîm," like great swaying Jacks-in-the-green, jostled by ; natives from Khordofan and Khartoum, Darfur and Dongola, mixed with the bean and lentil and wheat sellers from the Delta.   Once and again, glimpses were got of the river that gave their harbour city of Cairo (old Bûlâk) its birth. Long sloping yards, and gleaming patches of sail, peeped up above the mud banks at the landings.   The corn "runners," nearly naked, rushed round impossible corners, pushed their burdens into great hair sacks, took their beans to give up to the porter at the harbour-gate in token of the tale of sacks they had " run," popped another out of their mouths, which had been given them at the gate as a kind of tally, and away to the river's edge for a new burden.   Women, bare to the knee, holding their veils across their ugly faces, came up with their water-jars or " bellasses " balanced gracefully on their heads —all streaming and glistening in the sunlight.

Water-bearers clicked their cups, or offered "the gift of Allah " from the porous kullehs.   Tiny children, with golden beads and gay kerchiefs on their heads, patted camel-dung into cakes for fuel, and stuck them up in the sun upon the house walls to dry.   The money-changer chinked his coins and squinted at the passers-by, and a bullock-waggon got its solid wooden wheel into great ruts of mud and water, blocked the

whole street, stopped all the business ; but who cared
—it was the will of God, and the sun was shining !

At last Mohamed gave his last terrible " Ha-a-a "—
half wheeze, half groan, half sigh, half laugh—which is
the " Gee-up ! get along with you ! I am after you ! " all
in one, of the Cairene donkey-boy; and we halted
sharp at what might have been the respectable stable-
yard door of a suburban house.

" El antîkât " had been reached, and in another
moment we were crossing the gravelled court towards
the entrance of the Bûlâk Museum.

The building on our right, with its painted cornice
of blue, green, or red lotus panels, and its bunga-
low-looking façade, was in keeping with old Egypt.
We were going to see Pharaoh, and doubtless in his
great time this building of Bûlâk Museum would have
been thought worthy of a king.

On the right side, through the wooden gate by
which we had entered, there smiled on us the thick-
lipped animal-looking pugilist face of King Usertesen
I. of the twelfth dynasty, a colossus of rose-coloured
granite, with the royal " pshent," or conical head-dress
of royalty on his head; he who set up the pillar of
the thirty years, the obelisk at Heliopolis ; he who
styled himself thereon the " dispenser of life for
evermore " ; he who had died about 2400 B.C.

We pass on, and hardly wait to glance at the
four huge dark-grey figures of the lion-headed goddess

of passion, Secket Bast, holding on her knees the key of life that is death. The queer dog-headed and winged apes that once were held sacred as objects of worship at Abydos, the beautiful face of the Ethiopian queen in black basalt, the vast sarcophagi with their wonderful carving in bas-relief (the goddess of the next world holding the body equally balanced between earth and heaven) are hurried by, and we are just about to go up under the porch, with its serpent-circled orb of the disk of the sun blazoned above it, and its two granite figures of kings of the thirteenth dynasty, flanked again by rose-coloured statues of older kings, who stand up with their arms at "attention," and holding their long sceptres or shepherd staves by their sides, broad-cheeked, with caps, not crowns, upon their heads—such kings as Abraham knew—when our eyes suddenly catch sight of the blue Nile, beneath the sycamore trees beyond the garden wall, and we realise how with comparative ease the mighty sarcophagi—yea, and the mightier dead—were borne from far Abydos and from Thebes, and brought to rest here in the Bulâk sanctuary.

But, stay; ere you enter the shrine of antiquities, look back up the steps of the garden-ground, with its tree-ferns and palms mixing with the masts of the corn-ships in yonder harbourage.

There, on a pedestal of cement, shadowed by the waving fans of the palm, stands a grey, well-hewn plain sarcophagus. Four limestone sphinxes guard its base, behind rises up and overlooks the square box-looking tomb of slate-grey marble, a colossus of grey granite that bears (perhaps usurped upon it) the name of the Pharaoh we have come to see.

He who rests within that grey sarcophagus is Mariette Bey; those sphinxes from the avenue of Serapeum at Sakkara tell us as much. For it was Mariette Bey who brought to light their long-hidden sacred avenue of guardian sleep.

Yes, we are going to see Pharaoh, but I am not sure but that a mightier than Pharaoh rests there. Unsealer of great dynasties that were, recoverer of vast centuries, well does your body rest in this ante-chamber of recovered Egypt. There are those who follow you in your heroic work; there, behind the lattice, covered with its trailing plants, are tiny store-rooms, the shops of the idol menders and the anti-quity-restorers, and beyond, in a little study, where you, Mariette, worked of old, we shall find, if we send in our name and card, a welcome, and in a few moments we shall be talking with the kindest, gentlest guides to antiquity that the Bûlâk Museum boasts—Emile Brugsch Bey, brother of Henry Brugsch Bey, the historian. I had come to see Pharaoh, and here was the man who had brought him from the grave. I would learn the story from his lips. His faithful helper and associate, the little dark-

E

eyed man, who bowed me into his presence, Ahmad Effendi Kamal—he with one another could be trusted to assist Brugsch Bey in his dangerous undertaking, for they indeed carried their lives in their hands when they fetched Pharaoh from his eternal home.

Between the two I should surely learn something of the facts of the case. I did not learn them at one sitting, for Brugsch Bey has not only all the world of to-day, but all the worlds of the old Egyptian dynasties also, upon his shoulders. But it was my good fortune to see him several times, to go round the museum twice with him, and Effendi Kamal was often in and out of the different rooms, and always willing to answer questions.

The story of the find, then, was as follows. For a long time past tourists, who returned from Thebes to Cairo, brought with them scarabs, bits of papyrus, jewellery, cartonage, and the like, which so evidently belonged to the eighteenth and nineteenth dynasties— the era of Rameses I., Seti I., and Rameses II.—the great Rameses of the Bondage—that Mr. Maspero and Emile Brugsch Bey suspected there had been a great mummy find somewhere in the royal burial-place, " The Tombs of the Kings."

You will ask what is meant by the Tombs of the Kings. Briefly this :

At the western side of the great Theban plain rises up a vast mass of limestone rock, broken into

terraces. The man who has ever stood at Karnak,
and looked across the hill in the direction of the
Colossi and the Ramesseum, will remember how the
whole mountain mass seemed built by the hand of
giants into these vast terraces. Standing by the side
of the lofty obelisk, the loftiest in all Egypt, which
Queen Hātshepset, sister of Thothmes II., set up in
memory of her father in Karnak—(the throne or chair
of this wonderful queen was exhibited at the last Man-
chester Exhibition *) –the traveller sees, high up on
one of the terraces, the Temple of Dêr-el-Bahari.
That was the temple ante-chamber to her tomb; it
was not far from there that the great royal mummy
find was made.

However much the Theban kings might build
memorial temples in the Theban plain—as, for example, did Seti I., the father of the great Rameses,
when he built the Temple of Kurnah to the memory
of his father Rameses I., or Amenoph III., when he
raised the Amenopheum, whose sole remains to-day
are the two great colossi at Thebes, and as also did
the great Rameses when, in the mighty Hall of
Columns, which he blazoned with his wars against
the Kheta, he set among the calyx-tipped columns
and the lotus-bud capitals the pillar of his fame,
and the flower of his life's history; or, lastly, as did

---

* It is now in the British **Museum**.

Rameses III. when he designed the Temple of Medinet Habu—these temples were never tombs.

It is always to be remembered that these great kings took good care not to commit their bodies to these memorial shrines. After the lapse of 3000 years they were again to reappear upon the earth and re-inhabit their bodies. Those bodies, then, must not only be embalmed, but must also be most carefully guarded from harm; therefore in some out-of-the-way place, if possible, must their tombs be.

Now, it chanced that the huge limestone cliff of many terraces upon the western side of the Theban plain enclosed two desolate valleys. One of these opened on to the plain, and here, in pits and caves carefully hidden and protected by clever devices of block-fitting and angular shaft, the priests of old Thebes should lie in quiet; beyond, high up, well into the heart of the hills, where none but jackals would roam, in a valley where the sun beats mercilessly—where there is no shade except what the chameleon casts, where is no vegetation, and one realises what the breath of a furnace is—there, in the hidden valley of silence and heat, and death, should the bodies of the Theban kings lie till the Resurrection. The Nile might overflow, but here, in the valley of dry bones, in the limestone range, should these royal bodies lie in arid safety. War might flame at the hundred gates of the royal city below, and other conquerors break the peace of Thebes, but they should not disturb the rest of the Pharaohs. Here, even if they burnt to the ground the memorial temples of Hātshepset and Kûrnah, or shattered the hypostyle hall of the Ramesseum, these conquerors should never trouble the secret halls of the dead, high up in this burning valley of Bibân-el-Mulûk, as it is called to-day.

There, undisturbed, the bodies, wrapped in their thousand wrappings, encased in their double coffins, should sleep, and the priests alone should know the secrets of their abode in their caverns of eternity.

It is true that these cavern chambers in the tombs of the kings were carefully hewn—the kings of the eighteenth and nineteenth dynasties would at least see to this. Far in the burning valley of royal sleep they would each have their tomb-cavern cut. From Amenoph III. to the end of the twentieth dynasty, only the tomb of King Horus is missing.

Before they died, these kings doubtless clomb up the steep cliff by Dêr-el-Bahari, and entering the vale of Bibân-el-Mulûk, watched the sculptors and the decorators at their work—not hewing out or building a couple of rooms into a serdab or cupboard-chamber for the statue of the dead, as the old kings of the fifth to the thirteenth dynasty did, not covering the royal ceilings with the stars of heaven, and the walls with pictures of the everyday life of a great sporting gentle-

man farmer, as seen in the tomb of Tih or at the
mastăba of King Unas at Sakkara, or again in the tombs
of Beni hasân. No, but rather hewing a long tunnel
into the solid rock, with angles and stairways and
crooked passages, upon whose walls should be painted
the passage of the soul through its purgatorial suffer-
ings to the hall of blessedness ; upon whose doorways and portals should be depicted the puff-adders
spitting poison and flame, the guardians of the door of
heaven.

All these passages, with their pictures of the soul
passing through torment to rest, ended in a high resting chamber far in the hollow womb of limestone
mountain. There the soul should be re-born ; purified,
it should enter the bark of the sun, so the wall
pictures would tell us ; and there, waiting for its resurrection at the end of the 3000 years, the body of the
Pharaoh should lie beyond the hands of man or the
" unimaginable touch of time."

But how comes it about that so many of these tomb-
dwellings, whose mouths were carefully blocked till
they seemed one with the valley-side — to whose
mouths led such impossible little paths, over rough
plateau slopes—how comes it that these, when discovered from time to time, were found, as far as
mummies went, empty ? For instance, Bruce's tomb
in the Valley of the Kings, as it has been called, for all
its beauty of pictures, its harpers playing on the harps,

gave up no body of Rameses III. Belzoni's tomb, as
it has been re-named, for all its tableaux of the passage
of the sun through the hours of day and night, of Ra in
his bark of mystery and his battle with Āpepi, the
serpent of evil, hidden beneath the waves ; for all its
glorious sculpture, though it yielded the magnificent
white sarcophagus now in the Soane Museum, yielded
it empty of the body of the great King Seti I., for
which it had been hewn. The tomb of Rameses II.
had been examined, but it was empty. Archæologists
were puzzled : the bodies of these kings had been, and
were not. It was known from contemporary papyri
that the watching over the caverns of these tombs was
continuous. It was a legacy left from one king to
another, from one dynasty to another dynasty ; moreover, it was known that at certain periods the royal
mummies were partially unwrapped from their bandages to see that all was well, and wrapped up again
and restored to their rest.

A curious account of a State trial is in existence on
papyrus, of the fact that some priests had in the time
of Rameses II., the great Pharaoh, been found robbing
the dead ; and I have seen with my own eyes in the
Bûlâk Museum, so many hundred years after, a bit of
directest evidence against such roguery and sacrilege
in a beautiful bit of a mummy breastplate and ornament, from which the robbers had scraped all the
gold except in the sacred names and symbols, which

proves conclusively that the robbery and sacrilege had been done by the priests, who alone could know what sacred symbols should be untouched, and what secular gold ornaments might, without fear of penalties in the world to come, be taken.

Moreover, it was remembered that sometimes in the stormy day of revolution, or at the coming of new conquerors or new religions, the faithful servants of the buried kings would hurry off to the tombs in the valley of the Libyan Hill, whose secret hiding-places they alone knew, and remove by night, and re-bury in some less known, less celebrated tomb, the mummies of the mighty dead. The priests might be slain with the sword, and with them might die the secrets of the whereabouts, so that in a very few years the tombs of the Theban monarchs might, in that perplexing rocky ravine, be hidden from the hands or memories of men. Egyptologists were always on the look-out for the bodies of the eighteenth and nineteenth dynasty kings and queens.

Even supposing no revolution, no re-hiding for safety, research had shown how costly the keeping up of properly offered libations at the royal tombs must have been ; a low exchequer might induce any of the children of the great Pharaohs to compound for the sin of not keeping up the funeral feasts at the various rock chambers, by collecting all the dead into some one great mausoleum in the caverned hill.

It might be that even economy should have obliged a poorer Thebes to collect its great sleeping kings into one hall of rest, and one day that hall of rest should be found. But Thebes refused to part with its secret; nevertheless, as of old, Thebes produced its robbers of modern day.

Just beyond the Ramesseum, in some of the lines of tombs, four Arabs dwelt, whose family was Abd er-Rasoul; they were guides and jackal hunters. From about the year 1871 these men were known to bring and offer to travellers and tourists at Thebes the hands, the feet, and the ornaments of mummies. They dare not dispose of the bodies whole, for fear of the "kourbash"; but in their ignorance of hieratics they did dispose of some very interesting fragments of the ritual of the dead, some royal scarves of the nineteenth dynasty. A Mr. Colin Campbell brought to Cairo a beautiful royal ritual from Thebes,* and the Bûlâk authorities heard of it: there was evidently a good deal of body-snatching going on up at Thebes, and Mr. Maspero went thither. A conference with Daoud Pasha, the governor, ended in Maspero's offering of a large reward for any information that would lead to

---

* In addition to this book of the dead for Pi-net'em, there had also appeared a papyrus of Net'emet, a papyrus for Queen Hent-taiu, and an hieratic text on wood about some Uchabli figures belonging to Nessi-chensu.

the apprehension of the mummy finders and mummy sellers.

Still, the donkey-boys of Thebes, if they could get the traveller into a dark corner, would hand out from their dirty shirt-breast fronts, scarabs, and Osiris images, and bits of mummy bandage. Arrests were made, the bastinado was applied; but whenever a supposed culprit was had up, the women of Thebes, who were in the secret, and knew how the mummy find at Dêr-el-Bahari was the gold mine of Thebes, got round, and mocked at the men, and bade them keep *mum*, and so keep the mummies; dared them to split, cursed them for silly cowards, threatened them with death if they divulged; and the bastinado was in consequence ineffectual.

Abd er-Rasoul and his brothers were getting desperate. They would have sold Pharaoh for a song; and indeed in 1880 he was offered for sale, body and case, to an American, but refused by the Yankee as not being the genuine article. In 1881 grave suspicion fell upon the elder brother, Ahmad Abd er-Rasoul, as being in the secret. Mr. Maspero, with consent of Governor Daoud, had him arrested, and he was marched off to Keneh, and lay in prison for two months. The bastinado and the bribe Maspero had suggested were offered him alternately; he was threatened with death; but he was obstinately silent. Meanwhile the younger brother, Mohammed, thought half a loaf better than no bread, and determined, for the sake of Maspero's certain backsheesh, to get rid of the uncomfortable family secret, and the uncertain chances of any further loot from Pharaoh's tomb. He made a clean breast of the fact of the mummy-find, and gave the depositions to the Governor.

A telegram reached Cairo somewhere about July 1, 1881, and within a few hours my kind friend Emile Brugsch Bey, sub-curator of the Bûlâk Museum, with Tadros Moutafian and Ahmad Kamal, were on their journey of 500 miles up Nile to interview the now interesting Rasoul family, and to visit the newest find of Theban mummies—I was going to say, and to find Pharaoh, but this they had not hoped for; an important find they expected it to be, but they had not Seti I., or Rameses II., or Rameses III., or Queen Nefertàri in their thoughts, as they steamed up the river to Thebes.

Arrangements were made to meet Mohammed Abd er-Rasoul, the man of greed, at a high place in the limestone plateau near the ruins of the temple Der el-Bahari.*

On July the 5th, 1881, Brugsch Bey and his attendants climbed up the scorching, difficult cliff, and found, behind a huge mass of isolated rock looking as if a giant had flung it down from the cliff above, a

---

* The best distant view of the tomb mouth is from the path that leads past Dêr-el-Bahari to Dêr-el-Medinet, just before sighting the latter.

heap of stones ; apparently a heap at haphazard, really a very cleverly contrived bit of human invention to deceive. The spot was drear and unlikely beyond everything. " That's the place," said the sullen, sharp-eyed, savage-featured Ahmad Abd er-Rasoul; and in less time than it takes to write it, Brugsch Bey and his men were at work removing the blocks of stone and rubbish that filled a pit's mouth.

The well, six feet and a-half square, was found to be endless—or it seemed so to them in their impatience to explore. A palm tree was thrown across the well's mouth, a pulley and tackle rigged up, and quickly the work went forward under the burning noon.

At length the bottom, 40 feet down, was reached ; all the while Brugsch Bey and his assistant Ahmad were really in danger, for the fanatical robbers round them knew that the Bey was in reality going to be their ruin ; but his rifle was slung at his shoulder, and so the work went on.

At the bottom of the shaft they found an opening, running westward about 24 feet into the rock; on the right and left hand of the wall were curious hieratic inscriptions, possibly put there by the priests on the last date of their visit to see if Pharaoh was right. These have been photographed by Mr. Wilson, and are now in the hands of Mr. Maspero.

At the end of the 24 feet the passage turned sharply

to the right, and went northward. The hearts of the
explorers beat fast, for here they found a royal funeral
canopy in a heap on the ground, used perhaps last
when the coffin of one of the dead was floated down
to Thebes for burial, 1400 years before Christ.* Trin-
kets, alabaster boxes, canopic vases, bits of papyrus,
mummy cloth, and broken coffins strewed the way,
and a cluster of coffins nearly blocked it. The explorers were fairly staggered ; thence they crept for a
space, for the passage-way got very low, and they
found themselves at about 30 yards from the corner,
at the head of a rough-hewn stair or descent.

On they went. Boxes were seen piled by the walls,
filled, as they afterwards found, with the little statuettes
of Osiris—the Ushabti figures—libation jars, blue
enamelled drinking cups for the dead, and canopic
vases. On rushed Brugsch Bey, and at about 130 feet
from the opening to the well shaft he stood at the
entrance of a great mortuary chamber, 13 feet by
23 feet in floor space, and about 6 feet high. Their
torch showed that the whole room was packed roof
high with royal coffins ; and I who have seen the gold
and glitter and blue on Queen Nefertàri's beautiful
coffin, and the faces and the gilded heads and crooks

---

* This was the magnificent funeral-tent of Princess Isi-em-
Kheb, or more correctly, Uast-em-Khebit. A model of it to
scale is in the Bûlâk Museum pending the repair of original.

and the elaborate paintings and varnish of these wonderful double coffin cases, with their curious human faces peering up out of the rich inlay, as now exhibited in the Bûlâk Museum, of which Queen Ramaka and Uast-em-Khebit's coffins are good examples, can well understand that when Brugsch Bey's torch filled the dark with the reflection from eyes and hands of the illustrious dead, as depicted on their coffin lids, he felt so dazed that he went straight out of the tomb into the open air of the dying day, with the sort of feeling that on him hung a secret which, unless he lived till the morrow, might perish and leave the whole world the poorer. He feared to faint lest the secret should be unrevealed.

Here was a find of forty royal mummies at once! The chamber was the mortuary chamber of the Her-Hor family; Her-Hor was the founder of the priest-king dynasty, known as the twenty-first dynasty, that reigned in Thebes and Tanis between 1100 and 1000 B.C.; of this family alone, the bodies of two queens, two princesses, a scribe, and other royal and priestly personages, were discovered. They had been buried with all the sumptuous appendages of funeral repast and sepulchral toilet.

I saw in the Bûlâk Museum the wigs in the wig boxes, curled and frizzled, which one Queen Uast-em-Khebit hoped to wear at the Resurrection morn. Legs or shoulders of mutton, and chickens, mummified, for

the food of the soul in the next world ; offerings of
fruit, flowers, and garlands of acacia ; cups of blue
enamel, glass ointment bottles, and the like—these
were all found with the mighty dead in the Dêr-el-
Bahari cavern chambers, up on the lonely Libyan hills.

As I write, there rises up before me a vast outer
coffin of cartonage, in shape of a queen in full attire,
wearing a crown and the double plume ; her arms are
crossed upon her breast ; in each giantess hand she
holds the key of life ; and the blue enamel in the
corslet scales of her upper cloak still shines clear.

This vast giantess has been made out of thousands
of yards of finest linen, glued together, fold on fold, to
a thickness of two inches ; it stands up like one of the
Osiride pillars of the Medînet Habu Temple, and is
ten feet high if it is an inch.

What is this giantess ? She is a hollow dummy ;
she is simply the outer case of the beautiful coffin,
with its gold and blue, and the golden shining face
upon its cover, of Queen Nefertàri, of the eighteenth
dynasty ; and this was found in the passage of the
Dêr-el-Bahari, one of the forty royal mummy-cases of
the great discovery.

As I looked up at the giantess I did not wonder
how it took sixteen men to move her and her companion giantess from the mountain vault.

The find in the actual mortuary chamber of Her-
Hor was not as interesting as the find in the passage

that led to it. It was in this passage that the
mummies of the earlier dynasties, the seventeenth and
eighteenth, and of Seti and Rameses, were found, and
this alone is some evidence that the bodies of the great
dead had been removed hither for safety, or to save
expense, at some later date, from their original tombs.

The principal personages found among the forty
were a king and queen perhaps, of the seventeenth ·
dynasty, the Hyksos time, 2233 B.C. to 1733; four
kings and three queens of the eighteenth dynasty of
Thebes, 1700 B.C. to 1433; the three successive kings
of the nineteenth dynasty, 1400–1300 B.C.—namely,
the great Pharaoh of the Bondage, Rameses II., his
father, Seti I., and his grandfather Rameses I. One
body of a king of the twentieth dynasty was found.
But, as before stated, in the Her-Hor chamber were
discovered two queens, two princesses, a scribe, and
other notable personages of the twenty-first priest-
king dynasty that reigned between 1100 and 1000
B.C. As Brugsch Bey stood in that dark sepulchral
cavern-chamber and passage, he stood with the illustrious dead of seven centuries, none of whom were
living on this earth at a later date than 1000 B.C., some
of whom had fallen asleep and were embalmed as
much as 1700 years before Christ.

It was evident from the flowers and wreaths that
strewed the passage, that Mr. Maspero's backsheesh
had been only just in time. Close to his brother,

Thothmes II., in the passage, lay the sarcophagus or coffin of the great Napoleon of old Egypt, the warrior Thothmes III., of the eighteenth dynasty, great in name and deeds of war, but little in stature, for his mummy only measures five feet two inches. There in his coffin lay the conqueror of Syria, Cyprus, and Ethiopia, and probably had lain since 1600 years B.C. in an undisturbed shroud. But Abd er-Rasoul had been at work; the mummy was exposed to view; the bandages, with the litanies of the sun written upon them, had been torn and hacked about on the left breast; and the larkspur and acacia and lotuses, with the dried and mummified wasp which had crept in just as the embalmers had finished their work and laid their garlands on the dead, and that had lain there for some 3500 years, had been ruthlessly crushed by the hands of the robbers.

The next question was, How were these great dead to be removed to their final resting-place, the Bûlâk Museum? Steamers had been sent for to come up to Luxor. The bodies and coffin-cases must be lifted up the shaft, transported down the difficult cliff-side to the Theban plain; but the Nile was out in mid-plain, so they must be ferried across that, and then again borne on the shoulders of men to the Luxor river-side. All this Brugsch Bey saw in a moment: off to Luxor he and Kamal went, hired 300 Arabs in the night, and by earliest dawn were busy in the

F

removal and careful packing of the mummy-cases in matting and sailcloth.

"Set a thief to catch a thief" was Brugsch Bey's idea; and as he stood on guard at the pit's mouth he told off squads of Arabs to carry each mummy, with another squad to keep guard upon the robber carriers.

Night and day the work went on: in forty-eight hours the coffins had been hoisted to the pit's mouth; and after six days' hard labour under a July sun, the whole freight of sailcloth-sewn cases was at the Nile bank. For three days and three nights brave Brugsch Bey, Kamal, Moutafian, and a few trustworthy Arabs, one of whom might be seen any day in the Bûlâk Museum as a doorkeeper, kept watch over the find, amid as fanatical and frantically angry a set of ruffians and body-snatchers as ever Thebes and Luxor had produced.

It must have been a stirring sight as Brugsch Bey stood at the shaft-mouth, and watched the squads carrying their royal burdens across that vast Theban plain. He thus described it to Mr. Wilson:

"I shall never forget the scenes I witnessed, when, standing at the mouth of the Dêr-el-Bahari shaft, I watched the strange train of helpers, while they carried across that historical plain the bodies of the very kings who had constructed the very temples still standing, and of the very priests who had officiated in them: the temple of Hatasou nearest; away across from it,

Kûrnah ; further to the right the Ramesseum, where the great granite monolith lies face to the ground ; further south, Medînet Habu; midway between, Dêr-el-Medînet; and then the twin colossi, the vocal Memnon, and his companion ; then beyond all, more view of the plain; then the blue of the Nile and the Arabian hills far to the east; while slowly moving down the cliffs and across the plain, or in the boats crossing the Nile flood, were the sullen labourers carrying their ancient burdens.*

" As the Red Sea opened and allowed Israel to pass, so opened the silence of the Theban plain, and allowed the royal funeral procession to pass, and then—all was hushed again. Go up to Dêr-el-Bahari, and with a little imagination you will see it all spread out before you."

Emile Brugsch Bey is right.

But the steamers came at last, and the mummies were packed aboard ; and down the Nile, with the curses of Luxor upon their heads, and the hopes of all the antiquaries who knew of the find, as rich blessings upon their gallant undertaking, the Bûlâk party, with their convoy of ancient kings went.

The delay of those three days at Luxor was fatal to their peace. The news that Pharaoh was coming down

---

* A similar scene was witnessed last year, when, in February 1891, 163 bodies of the priests and priestesses of Amen were borne from the mummy-pit below the temple of Hâtshepset to the river-banks at Luxor under the care of M. Grébaut.

Nile had got on ahead, and Mr. Brugsch Bey told me that one of the most striking things in the whole journey, to his mind, was the way in which there arose from all the land of Egypt " an exceeding bitter cry," and women wailing and tearing their hair, men casting dust above their heads, came crowding from the villages to the banks, to make lamentation for Pharaoh.

Yes, the whole heart of Egypt and the old love for the mighty kings of the splendid days of old, was deeply moved, and, as in the days more than 3000 years ago, with wailing and great weeping, the funeral barge had carried the dead kings up Nile to their sleep among the Theban hills ; so to-day, with wailing and weeping and gnashing of teeth, and all the signs of a national lamentation, did the bodies of the mighty Pharaohs sail swiftly down through a land of mourning and sorrow, from their long repose in the Theban valley of the dead, to their final rest at Cairo beside the shining Nile.

I had read in the *Academy* of July 3rd, 1886, the very startling and accurate account of the unwrapping of the mummies of Rameses II. and Rameses III. which took place at the Bûlâk Museum, June 1st, 1886. There, in the presence of His Highness Tewfik Pasha, Khedive of Egypt, and their excellencies Moucktar Pasha Ghazi, High Commissioner of the Sultan, Sir Drummond Wolff, Her Majesty's

Consul, and other great persons, M. Gastin Maspero, the director of the antiquities of Egypt, and his subordinates, Messrs. Brugsch Bey and Bouriant, unrolled at nine o'clock in the morning the royal mummies brought from Dêr-el-Bahari, and marked in the catalogue Nos. 5229 and 5233.

There was more of interest than at first sight attached to the unwrapping of the royal mummy No. 5233, for though the coffin had been found in close proximity to, and company with, the coffins of Seti I. and Rameses I., and though the coffin-lid bore the nomen and prenomen of the illustrious Sesostris, it had been suggested by some Egyptologists that Rameses XII., of the twentieth dynasty, a man of no great noteworthiness, bore the similar divine name or cartouche as the great Rameses the Second, of the nineteenth dynasty. This coffin might contain the lesser notable's body, after all. The savants further pointed out that the coffin-case was of the Osirian type of the twentieth or twenty-first dynasty; so that, as the royal assemblage gathered round coffin No. 5233 on the 1st of July 1886, though Maspero was fully persuaded that the great Pharaoh's body lay before them, enveloped in its pink-coloured and yellow cerements, there was just enough element of doubt about it, to render his task intensely interesting as a work of identification, apart from the fact of the unveiling of a royal monarch.

The *procès verbal* of the dates on the coffin-lid
pointed to the mummy being the mummy of the
great king. It had been written in black ink on the
sycamore coffin-case, and gave the years six and sixteen of the royal or high priest Her-Hor Siamun, and
the tenth year of the royal or high priest Pinotmou
I.; another date, of the sixteenth year of the royal
priest Pinotmou I., was traced on the first cerecloth or
wrapping, just at the breast. The Khedive's attention
was called to the inscription ; he nodded assent, and
the unwrapping went forward. Beneath the first
envelope was discovered a band of cloth, wrapped
round and round the body, then a second envelope
or shroud, sewn and kept in its place by narrow bands
from space to space ; next came two layers of small
bandages and then a piece of fine linen, stretching
from head to foot ; on this was painted, in red and
black, a representation of the goddess of creation out
of nothing, Nouit or Neith, as prescribed by the ritual
of the dead.   The goddess in profile unmistakably
resembled the delicate features of Seti I. the father
of Rameses II., as made known by the bas-reliefs of
Thebes and Abydos. This was proof, not positive, but
looking very much as if the great son of Seti I. lay
within. A band of brand-new material had been placed
beneath this amulet of the goddess Nouit; then
came a kind of quilt, of pieces of linen folded in squares
and stuck together by the bituminous preparation the

embalmers had used.　There was considerable excite-
ment amongst the bystanders.　This last covering was
removed, and lo! in less than a quarter of an hour
from the commencement of the unwrapping, appeared
from beneath its many cerements the great Sesostris
himself, who had been embalmed with such care, and
wrapped up so laboriously, 3186 years ago.

As we passed up and into the vestibule of the
Bûlâk Museum, Arab watchmen grinned and said:
" Ramses Kebeêr Khawaja?" ("Do you want to see
the great Rameses, Sir?") "Ramses Deux henâk"
("This is the way to the second Rameses"), said another
Arab in broken Arabic; and I followed as in a dream.

I entered the grand vestibule, but looked not on
my left, neither at the rose-coloured granite statue
of Sebak em Saf, king of the thirteenth dynasty, nor
on the admirably cast lion of bronze which served
King Apries as one of the stair ornaments of his
throne, in the twenty-sixth dynasty.　I looked not on
the right, to the serpentine statue, gleaming as though
it were bronze, of the human-breasted hippopotamus
in form of a goddess Thoueris, who, it was believed,
would superintend the bringing of life again into the
bodies of the dead, when they rose from their mummy
shrouds.　I gazed not up at the subtle and refined
face in black basalt, half proud, half cruel, of young
Meneptah, the Pharaoh of the Exodus, wearing the
double crown, and the limestone portrait-bust of

broad-browed and beautiful Queen Taia, the wife of
Amenophis III., of the eighteenth dynasty, close by.
I regarded not the fat, pulpy, animal-looking face of
Khâi, who crouched, in two squatting statues, chin on
knee, as large as life, on either side the doorway of the
grand vestibule—not even though I knew that this
same Khâi was guardian of the treasures in the
mortuary chapel of Rameses' II., the great Pharaoh I
was soon to stand before.

So, with heart beating fast, into the grand vestibule
I went. A beautiful statue of alabaster, lightly draped
and life-size, through which the sunlight fairly shone,
of Queen Ameneritis, a sister of Sabaco, and wife of
Piankhi, of the twenty-fifth dynasty, with left hand
clasping to her breast a lotus-flower, her right hand
hanging at her side and holding a key, would have at
any other time detained me. On I went. Upon my
left stood the famous wooden statue of the Shêkh el
Beled, naked to the waist, and bare-legged, with his
lustrous quartz eyes glittering from his broad, good-
tempered face of shining sycamore, holding a long
wand-like staff in his hand, knobby as the day it was
cut, put there in the time of the pyramids, 3600 B.C.

No; I could not look at him now—I was going
to see Pharaoh. Right in front of me sat, in his
marvellous, masterful repose, the heroic statue of
Chephren, the founder of the second pyramid that bears
his name; there, with his right hand clenched upon

his knee, and holding the little scroll that proves him
scholar and scribe, bare to the waist and bare of leg,
wearing his ample cap or wig, with side flaps de-
pendent over his brawny shoulders—there sat the
man as he looked in pride and power, upon the
people of his day.

There, on his throne, or throne-chair of state, with
the "psam," or symbol of sovereignty of Upper and
Lower Egypt, the intertwined lotus flower and papyrus rush, sculptured in high relief upon the sides of
the chair, with the hawk, or holy bird of Horus,
perched behind him, stretching out its wings about
his head in token of divine love and protection,
Chephren seemed to command me to stop and gaze
upon him. "If you will not gaze on me, who gazed
upon the builders of the pyramids, at least," the great
statue seemed to say, with a kind of scornful smile
upon his face of calm content, " gaze upon the rock
out of which I have been hewn. Behold this diorite
grey and green. Have you any men alive on earth
now, or any tools with stubborn enough a temper to
carve and model muscle and sinew thus in adamant."

I almost heard myself answering my own interroga-
tive of scorn : " O, king, live for ever. Men were
giants in thy days." But I could not stay. I was
going to see Pharaoh.

Queen Aahhotep's wondrous jewellery glittered near
—she whose vast Osiride coffin, ten feet high, I should

presently see in the next room.   It was wondrous, that jewel display ; it would be wondrous for work-manship in any display of crown jewels of to-day.   It had been buried with her who was mother of Aahmes, the founder of the eighteenth dynasty at Thebes, 1700 B.C., and who had been the wife of Amenophis I., who succeeded Aahmes.

But I could not gaze : I was going to see Pharaoh.

On into the "Salle Funéraire," as it was called, I went.   I knew that round its walls were the house-hold furniture, the tables, the chairs, the writing-desks of Abraham's time ; that such agricultural im-plements as he handled were here, that baskets of fruit such as he ate were in absolute preservation of dried fruitage on the shelves.

On my right, too, was that famous tomb-chamber prepared for the Theban grandee Horhotpou in the dim eleventh dynasty, more than 2500 B.C., with all its painting fresh upon it, with its calendar and tables of offerings as legible as when they were painted. But I went straight forward.

Before me was the open portal of the "Salle des Momies royales," and I was going to see Pharaoh. With a curious feeling of awe and expectancy, I gained the room—the entire roof supported on two pillars.   It was well lit from above ; seemed to be, in part, divided into two by projecting walls on east and west.

Against these partition walls stood up the great solid wooden-looking, in reality hollow, papier-mâché images of Queen Aahotpou,* wife of Amenophis I., and mother of Aahmes of the eighteenth dynasty, and Queen Aahmes-Nefertàri, wife of Aahmes or Amosis, the founder of the dynasty and mother of Aahotpou.

One did not wonder that the carriers from the well-hole at Dêr-el-Bahari had groaned beneath the burden of these giantesses, with their crowns and double plumes standing now ten feet high ; but we remembered how the mummy of one inside the coffin, which was inside the giant cartonage, had given us a knowledge of how the jewellers of those old days worked in precious stones and silver and gold, and one could not regret that the Theban mummy stealer had lost his sweat and his booty at once.

Cases fronted with glass, filled with the finds of wigs, statuettes, cups, flowers, emblems, inside the mummy coffins, ran up the bays right and left of the giantesses.

All round the room, above the shelves and reaching to the ceiling, coffin-cases, with their quaint human-looking heads, and painted wigs, and glass eyes, and golden hands projecting from their painted and enamelled coffin-lids, looked down upon me. Then immediately, high up on my right as I entered the

---

* Spelt also Ahhotpou, Aah-hotep, and Aāh-hetep.

room, carved out of plain sycamore, with the hands,
well-modelled, crossed on his breast, holding a four-
corded flail, painted red, in his right hand, and crook
of office, painted green, in his left, with thin plaited
beard and heavy eyebrows, full lips, nose a little
retroussé, ears large, prominent and bored for jewellery,
and with an inscription in hieratics of black ink, and
two cartouches, who should be looking with dark
enamel-eyes out of his smooth Osirian-shaped coffin
lid but an image of Pharaoh—the great Pharaoh I had
come to see.

I had been made familiar with some of the royal
cartouches, and at once recognised these.   The prenomen Ra-User-ma Sotep-en-ra, and the nomen Ra-
Meri-Su-meri-Amen. Ah! favourite of Ammon, beloved
of the sun, it is you I have come so far to seek ! And
though this coffin-lid is, by its shape, not earlier in
date than the twenty-first dynasty, its absence of all
attempt at ornament tells a tale.   When Pharaoh was
last coffined, 1000 years before Christ, the coffin-
makers made haste, for the name of the great Egyptian Rameses II. had ceased to be the name of a
god, and decency, not honour, was due to his mortal
remains.

Beneath this coffin-lid, and ranged as close as
possible along the southern side of the room at my
back, were the splendid coffins and sarcophagi of
lustrous enamel and wonderful painting from Dêr-el-

Bahari, in various degrees of preservation. I did not
ask whose they were; my guide had his face set as
though the Pharaoh I had come to see lay on the
northern or further side of the room, and simply with-
drawing his finger from pointing up at the coffin-
lid of sycamore, he gave a click as he said "Ramses
Deux." I passed forward into the sanctum, the part
of the room beyond the pillars, beyond the bays,
beyond the giant Osirian cartonages; yet had I not
been under a spell I must have stopped in the middle
of the room, for there in the centre of the nearest
division was a funereal bed, a kind of open litter
of wood-work, resting upon two lions, whose heads
were painted green, whose tails were long and up-
curled, and whose feet made as it were the feet of the
litter.

Within the balustrades, upon the litter lay the
mummy of the daughter of Prince Takelot, of the
twenty-third dynasty, a princess and priestess of
Ammon; but it was evident at a glance that the forty-
four seven-inch balustrades of red and green and blue,
which bore the cornice and frieze of blue and yellow,
banded with green, red, blue, and yellow bands, was
much earlier in date, and by its appearance was evidently intended to represent the decorations and
shape of a Theban tomb of the eleventh dynasty,
and such Mr. Brugsch Bey told me it was indeed.
On such funeral beds, before embarkation on the

funeral barge, lay, beneath the wreaths and offerings of lotus and acacia, the noble dead in the days that were 2000 years before Christ.

But I was going to see Pharaoh ; and on I went. But again I stopped, for beyond it, under a large glass case, was an exact reproduction, on a scale of one-third, of the leather funeral tent or canopy of the mummy Uast-em-Khebit, of the twenty-first dynasty, which was found near her coffin, and which must do duty here till the original of dyed leather has been thoroughly restored.

At a rough guess, the original must have been about 10 feet 6, by 7 feet 6 wide, and 8 feet high ; and glorious must it have appeared on the morning they rowed Uast-em-Khebit, the mother of Pinotem III., of the twenty-first dynasty, to her royal rest, her eternal home among the Theban hills.

The top of the funeral tent seemed to be striped with stars and devices that looked like daisies of yellow and pink on a blue-green ground ; a band of six-winged hawks of the sun ran round. The sides and ends looked like a patchwork of pink and green chessboard squares ; these draperies hung down from a cornice made of scarabs, holding in their arms pink fans and lotus flowers in squares.

In front, on the frieze as it were, gazelles crouched by a palm cluster, with lotus flowers about their necks ; at the back, on the bottom of the curtain, shone out a hawk of gold, 12 inches across, and on the curtains either side, by way of ornament, were four scarab panels, with five uræus basilisks alternate.

But all this closer observation was made by me at a later time. I could only, in my impatience, get a rough glance of a square tent in miniature, flat-roofed, with drapery straight down, a cube of pink and green patchwork, with colours fresh and wonderful, more like five painted chessboards, set up in form of a box upside down, than anything else.

I could not the least realise then the wonderful patience of Messieurs Bouriant and Brugsch Bey, the restorers of the original, and makers of this model in all its exactness as to scale and colour.

Neither funeral bed of the eleventh nor funeral tent of the twenty-first dynasty could impress me as they afterwards did; for I was going to see Pharaoh.

I was going to see Pharaoh, and stood in the doorway of the Salle des Momies—nay, I was in his audience chamber now. Round me as I looked—or rather on three sides of me—lay, with their feet towards me, what might have been twelve coffins. They were in reality twelve great cases of pitch-pine, with glass lids, inside which the coffins and the mighty dead now lay. These glass coffin-containers were all covered with palls, as it seemed of drab cloth : a curious feeling of an inquest came over me, and I felt as if I were in a death-chamber, about to gaze upon twelve dead bodies ;

and yet a voice within me seemed to say : " They are not dead, they sleep : do not wake them."

Neither I nor the guide spoke. What a presence-chamber it was. Beneath these shrouds, on my right, lay nearest me, Pinotem II., the fourth priest-king of the twenty-first or Her-Hor dynasty. Next, Makeri· (Ramaka) with her little child, a pink grey bundle, at her feet—poor queen, she died in childbirth. Next, Nebseni, the famous priest-scribe of the Her-Hor dynasty; next, Notemhit, or Netemhut, the proud mother of Her-Hor, the founder of this line of priest-kings, in whose family-vault these Pharaohs of the eighteenth and nineteenth dynasties had been so marvellously preserved to us.

Not one of these mummies lived before 1100 B.C., or after 1000 B.C.

Immediately in front of me lay four other illustrious dead in their glass-covered drab-palled coffin-cases : Aahmes I. or Amosis, the friend of the gallant old pug-faced admiral who bore his name, and who fought his ships of old so bravely, the "Calf," and "The North," and "The going up into Memphis" ; Aahmes, the founder of the eighteenth dynasty, date 1700 B.C., the conqueror at Avaris and Sherohan, the warrior of a twenty-two years' war, the restorer of the rightful line of Pharaohs after the expulsion of the Shepherd Kings. Next to him, on his left as I looked, Rameses II. ; next to him Seti I., his father, 1366 B.C., both of the

nineteenth dynasty ; next him Thothmes II., king of
the eighteenth dynasty, B.C. 1600. To complete the
horseshoe on the left side of the room we must name
Amenophis I., who succeeded Aahmes, the second king
of the eighteenth dynasty, 1666 B.C.

Next to him, on his left as I gazed, lay Rameses
III., the founder of the twentieth dynasty, 1200 B.C.
Next to him, Princess Nessi Chensu, of the twenty-
first dynasty ; and last, and next to her, Raskenen *
Tiouâquen, the man who fought and fell for liberty
in the war of independence that eventually banished the
Hyksos somewhere in the seventeenth century B.C.

All this was not, of course, known to me as I
approached the mighty Pharaoh where he lay. I had
a general idea that I was in the presence of royalty
that had fallen asleep between 1680 and 1000 years
before Christ. The thought staggered me. " Rameses
Kebeêr henak " (" Pharaoh, the great one, is there "),
said the swarthy guide ; and with a look of reverence
upon his fine face, he moved the coverlet and pall a
little from the glass, slowly turned it back, and let it
slide, of its own weight, off the sloping frame ; and
there, full length within his coffin, looking up at me
with his proud gaunt face that had outfaced the world,
with his withered hands across his breast almost in
attitude of prayer, the mighty king, in his great

---

* Known also as Seqenen-Ra.

G

slumber, lay; and I knew what it was to be in the presence of him before whom Egypt trembled, and the Hittites fled, and from whom the Israelites, bowed down in bitter bondage in the brickfields of Rameses and Pitûm, cried unto the Lord their God. There A-nakhtu, the great warrior as he was called, was taking his rest—he who had escaped from the Hittites when " he was all alone and none other was with him," who had burst through the blazing faggots of reeds that so nigh consumed his royal tent at Pelusium that day his treacherous brother made him his guest, and would have murdered him as he slept, full of wine, —he who had faced death in so many ways was now alone, was dead; but dead, he yet defied corruption.

The coffin wherein the great Pharaoh rested, was about two inches thick, less thick and much less deep and less large than the one near it, in which his father Seti lay.

Washed with pinkish colour outside, it was within painted with a yellow wash of ochre, its bottom roughly daubed with pitch. Made, as all the Osirian coffins are made, more or less to fit the body, this was no exception to the rule; but at a glance, after contrasting it with the usual elaborately ornamented and decorated insides of coffins of royalty, with their winged hawks, their " Uta " eyes, their emblems of the guardians of the soul, their goddess Neiths, their priests in attitude of offering, and the like, it was quite plain that

this was not the original coffin in which, somewhere
about the year 1300 B.C., the Pharaoh Rameses II.
had been laid, but one that had been made in haste,
and that by appearance and shape, was as late as the
twenty-first dynasty. Two inscriptions in hieratics
bear out this. First, we learn from these, that the
official inspectors of the tombs, in the sixth year of
Her-Hor, founder of the twenty-first dynasty, visited
the royal tomb 1100 B.C. There, for two centuries
the body had probably lain undisturbed, but it is
clear that about this time, as we learn from the
Abbott-papyrus, the tombs of the royal kings were
being looted. The " Amherst "-papyrus details a full
confession of a tomb-breaker and body-snatcher of
this date. "We found the august king," says this
penitent thief, "with his divine axe beside him, and
his amulets and ornaments of gold about his neck;
his head was covered with gold, and his august
person was entirely covered with gold; his coffin was
overlaid with gold and silver within and without, and
incrusted with all kinds of precious stones." What,
think you, did this forerunner of the rogue Abd er-
Rasûl do? Hear his own confession : "We took the
gold which we found upon the sacred person of this
god, as also his amulets and the ornaments which were
about his neck, and the coffins in which he reposed."

It is more than probable that the tomb-inspector
of Her-Hor found that the coffin of Rameses II. was

being thus tampered with, for we find that ten years after that first official inspection, a commission of priests visits the coffin of Rameses II., which is no longer in his own eternal home, but in the tomb of his father Seti I. On an inscription on the coffins of Seti and Rameses II. it is stated that the bodies of the kings—father and son—are unharmed, but for safety's sake they deem it expedient to move the mummies to the tomb of Queen Ansera, of the eighteenth dynasty. But again the robbers got wind of it. In ten years' time, in the twentieth year of Pinotem I.—that is, in about the year 1023 B.C.—this body, on which we are gazing, was removed for security's sake to the tomb of Amenophis I., the second king of the eighteenth dynasty, who had died 1635 B.C.

It rested here for six years, and then, as we learn from hieratics on one of the breast bandages of the royal mummy, Pharaoh was removed for the fourth time, and carried to his father's tomb in the Valley of the Kings. He was not found there after all, but in the family vault of Her-Hor, as we know, at Dêr-el-Bahari. Is it to be wondered at, then, that this rough coffin-case, in which the great king lies, is not the original coffin, but shows signs of haste and expediency in its making?

Now, look at the mummy : he fairly fills the coffin length—yes, though he has shrunk, as all dead bodies do, as old men are shrunk before they die, he measures still more than six feet, as he lies. He must have in life been six foot two, or six foot three, at least.

A life-guardsman in mould, in very truth he must have seemed. Withered though the muscles on his neck to his spinal column's girth be, what a length of neck it must have seemed! And swathed though he be in his yellow mummy-cloth shroud of well-woven linen, yet his shoulders are bare to view. What mighty shoulders they were! What breadth of chest must have been his!

I gazed upon Pharaoh. I saw him standing in his chariot once again on that glorious battle-field of Kadesh, by the river Orontes, when he arose, as the contemporary court-poet Pen-ta-ur tells us in his forcible epic, like Menthu, god of war, " and urged on his steeds, whose names were ' Triumph in Thebes,' and ' The Divine Mother.' None dared follow ; he was alone, and none other with him ; and lo ! he was encircled by the Khetan host—2500 chariots were around him, and countless hosts cut off the way behind."

" Not one of his friends, not one of the captains of his chariots, not one of his knights was with him ; his bodyguard had abandoned him." And I seemed to see the great warrior lift himself in his chariot, and hear him cry unto the lord his god in passionate prayer : " Where art thou, my Father Amen ; has ever a father forgotten his son ? Shall it be for nothing that I have dedicated to thee many and noble temples? My warriors have deserted me; but what are multitudes of men against me? More to me is thy power than myriads of men. On thee, Father Amen, do I call."

A light seemed again to come into the dead warrior's face as he felt his prayer was heard, in the temple of the god at Hermonthis. "Amen heard his voice, and came to his cry. He reached his hand to him, and the warrior shouted for joy. He called out to him : 'I have hastened to thee, Rameses, my well-beloved. The brave heart I love, it has my blessing; I am with thee ; I am he, thy Father—the sun-god Ra. My hand is with thee.'"

"All this," so sang Pen-ta-ur the bard, "came to pass ;" and we, as we look upon this great king in his coffin now—we can see him, in the fury of that desperate charge, rushing on his foes like a flame of fire. See those long arms, and that powerful frame swayed in the terrible contest, and dealing the blows of a giant right and left, while the Hittites fell like chaff before the feet of his horses, and we can realise how terrible, how like a god, he must then have seemed, of whom the poet sang :

" I was changed at the voice of Amen, being made like the God Menthu in my might. I hurled the dart with my right hand, I fought with my left ; none dared to raise his hand against me. They could not shout, nor grasp the spear ; their limbs gave way beneath them. I made them fall into the water, as the crocodiles fall into the stream. Each cried to his fellow, ' It is no mortal man who is against us, it is Seti the mighty—it is the God of War.'"

I think, as one realises the statue of Rameses II. laid in his long coffin, as one looks on his face in the sleep that knows no breaking, one can imagine the awe and terror with which, when roused to passion or rebuke, this god incarnate, as he was believed to be, must have been invested, at court or camp, on throne or battle-field. Terrible as his favourite lion "Semen-Kephtu-f," or "Tearer to Pieces," must have seemed as it lay at his throne-steps or ramped to battle at the chariot-wheel of his royal master, more terrible must have seemed the lord of lions and the lion-city Heliopolis, the son of the sun, the favourite of Ammon, as with his reins girt round about his waist, to leave his great arms free for bow and spear, Rameses II. rushed into battle and thundered his commands.

Let us look at his face closely. In colour it is light brown, almost yellow in fairness. The head is narrow, and is what we should call *dolicho-cephalic*— that is, the head is thin and projects far backward— the length from nose to back of the skull is very considerable. There is a swelling out of the skull over the ears : I expect the believer in bumps would say that Pharaoh was probably mischievous ; the forehead is high, but so far from being straight or prominent, it retreats, and must have in life taken much from the dignity of the face.   The eyes are nearer than I had expected to see them—nearer together, as I found out afterwards, than his father Seti's eyes; the eyebrows, to judge by the sparse white hairs that still remain, must have been thick; certainly if we may judge from a gem which gives us the portrait of his Mesopotamian mother, Queen Tua, his eyebrows were his mother's eyebrows.   Bald though he was, on the crown of his head, he must have had abundance of hair, by what remains to him at the back.   It is true it appears now yellow, but this is partially owing to the stains of the embalming unguents; and the old man, of near a hundred summers, must have gone to his grave with a circlet of snow-white hair, snow-white eyebrows, and a snow-white moustache upon his upper lip.

But it was not in his head that lay his strength, nor in his brow, nor in his eyes.   No; Pharaoh's strength of face lay and lies in the nose, the ears, the mouth, and the chin.   The nose, unlike his father's and his mother's, is Napoleonic—a beaked Bourbon nose.   Truly the bandages of the mummy shroud have pressed upon the tip of the nose, and exaggerated the eagle-beakedness, but it must have been *the* feature of the great Pharaoh's face—this great, strong aquiline nose.   The ears are large and flat—larger than were the ears of any of the royal mummies I

examined ; great elephant-flappers of ears, that stood
out from the head. I have often seen such ears
associated with love of music, and I do not believe
that the poets Pen-ta-ur and Amenemapht would have
had so much encouragement given them under
Rameses II. had not this Pharaoh loved the sound
of the harpers. The ears had been bored for jewels,
but both lower lobes had been broken. The cheek-
bones were high and prominent, and gave perhaps, in
life, a certain haughty, overbearing strength to the less
powerful upper part of the face. I was struck by the
length from the nose to the lip. As for the mouth,
it had once had lips full fleshed, fuller-fleshed certainly than the lips of Seti, his father, and though
the mouth was a little brutal, I should think, in life,
it did not give me the impression of sensualism or
want of refinement. It was a strong mouth, it was a
stubborn mouth ; it seemed a mouth of contempt and
self-will, a mouth of pride ; but not necessarily, a mouth
of animalism.

The teeth were white—much worn and brittle, but
wonderful teeth for a centenarian, and well-set. The
strength of the face was emphasised by the chin,
square and massive, with great length from front of
chin to ear, full of power and force ; the pride of the
face seemed doubled by the set of that chin ; there
were upon it slight traces of a beard of coarse hair,
that may have grown after death. The face was worn

and thin: what old man's of near a hundred years would not be? There were slight traces of wrinkles upon the brow.

The father of a hundred and nineteen children— fifty-nine sons and sixty daughters, as the outer wall of the Temple of Abydos tells us—he was the pos sessor of many concubines, and of at least four lawful wives; we might have supposed that the cares of a family would have worn his face, if the cares of all Egypt and the Egyptian court-life of sixty-seven years—for the monuments expressly tell us he did reign sixty-seven years—had not left their mark upon it. But though a side face or profile view of the great king, as obtained by a photograph, gives a look of fatigue and a certain gladness to be at rest, I could not, do what I would, see in that proud, obstinate face of the warrior-king in his shroud before me, any-thing that looked like a yielding to the weight of years; there was a kind of " What is all this to me? Am I not son of the sun—Rameses, favourite of Ammon? Shall not my years endure as long as the sun shineth in his strength? Will not my sun that sets, arise in the morning?" Monsieur Maspero wrote the day he unwrapped the great Sesostris (you will find it in the *Academy* of July 3, 1886): " In fine, the mask of the mummy gives a very sufficient idea of what the king was in life: an expression not very intellectual, perhaps rather animal, but of pride and obstinacy, and

with an air of sovereign majesty, still to be seen
through all the grotesque appearance of the embodiment." I did not find this animalism was in the face;
rather—as I note on looking at my diary of several
audiences of the great Pharaoh in his death-chamber
—I felt that there was a certain refinement about a
face whose weakness lay in the forehead, whose might
lay in the chin and in the eagle nose.

As for the rest of the body, still might be seen the
wound in the side, whence the embalmer's hand
withdrew the viscera at the time of death. The
thighs and legs were thin, the feet large and flat. I
was struck with the coarseness or thickness of the
ankles, but got therefrom an idea of the robust
strength of this Pharaoh, whose natural force was
unabated when the death-hour came, and who could
probably then, as he did in the Hittite battle, stand
alone. His feet had been, after the fashion of the
time, rubbed red with henna, and as I looked on the
hands—laid peacefully across one another on his breast,
the left hand over the right—I noticed what long
hands and fingers they were; how neatly, too, the
nails had been cut into points, the middle finger of
the left hand being specially noticeable, and how
carefully they also had been dyed with the rich red
henna-stain before they had been packed up, finger by
finger, in the swathing bands of eternity, the linen of
the embalming priests.

Ah! how one wished to question the mighty monarch; but he was silent—his mouth stopped with the embalmer's black paste that was put there 3187 years ago.

And this is the " Bull in the land of Rutennu," " the Hawk of the Sun," " A-nakhtu the Warrior," he who conquered Kush and led into captivity the people of Shashu, the hero of the battle against the Kheta, who washed his heart, as the poet puts it, in the blood of his enemies, the architect of the city of the sun Heliopolis and the temple-city Rameses, the founder of Memphis with its bull-arena and its glorious temple to Ptah or Vulcan, the beautifier of Abydos, the gold-digger in Nubia, the well-digger in the land of Kush, the brickmaker at Pitûm and canal-designer in the field of Zoan, the endower of libraries for Thebes, the mighty builder of the Ramesseum, the giver of a hundred temples to the gods in the land of Egypt. He who set up his mighty double images of limestone at Memphis, his red colossal statue on the Theban plain, who had himself painted at Abu Simbel and Abydos, and carved wonderfully at Tanis and on the façade of the Temple of Hathor at Abu Simbel, who sits on the southern colossus at the great temple of Abu Simbel, who smiles upon us from the rosy syenite, that once adorned the Ramesseum, in the Egyptian court of the British Museum. The inscriber of his name and deeds upon the obelisk which stands above our London river; who calls himself thereon, boastfully but truly enough, "The guardian of Egypt, chastiser of foreign lands, dragging foreigners of the southern nations to the great sea, and the foreigners of northern nations to the four poles of heaven." The recreator of Egypt in a very real sense, who, in his prayer to the god of Memphis, said, "I have cared for the land in order to create for thee a new Egypt," of whom the scribe at Memphis wrote, "All are as one, to celebrate the powers of this god, even of King Rameses Meri-Amen, the war-god of the world."

There in his coffin, life's battle won, life's long work done, lies the war-god and the peace-god of Egyptian history. A man who in his lifetime dared to associate himself with the great gods Ptah and Ammon and Horus; father of the princess Meris, who drew Moses from the bulrushes; the oppressor of the children of Israel: we who bow the knee before the God he knew not, how can we not be impressed with the thought of such pride in such ashes now before us?

Yet he served his time, prince of learning and father of the arts, great in peace as he was great in war, for a whole generation would know him more as an acute administrator than as a warrior-king. And had this Pharaoh not lived and reigned his sixty-seven years, the world would have been the poorer. We feel what that shrivelled, gaunt body in the coffin there aimed

at and honoured, as vital powers to kindle and restrain
us still. As I gazed for the last time upon that proud
forcible face, the gratitude and strength of the limestone colossus among the palms of Memphis; the
gentleness and affection portrayed in the statue by
the side of his wife at the right of the façade of the
Temple of Hathor at Abu Simbel; the superiority
and calm carelessness of might upon the face of the
southern colossus at the great temple of Abu Simbel;
the fire in his face in that war-chariot at the Hittite
battle, as seen pictured at the Ramesseum; the thought-
fulness, mingling with scorn, of the colossal face at
Tanis—all seemed to come together and live again in
the withered cheeks of the tall old king. The mummy
of Sesostris, at the end of his 3187 years, justifies all
the chief portrait-sculptors of his day as being true,
and makes us, who have seen Pharaoh again in the
flesh, acknowledge, at the same time, that this was indeed Rameses, the Great One.

What a resurrection from the dead it all is ! How
the centuries run back upon themselves as we gaze !
One of the very oars, or paddles, with which they rowed
his body across the sacred lake, to his burial in the hill
above the Theban plain, is there within that cabinet
close by; and there too are the blue lotus flowers—their
colour still faint upon them—with which they gar-
landed the dead king, and decked him for the tomb.

CHAPTER IV.

SETI, THE FATHER OF PHARAOH THE GREAT:
AN HISTORICAL SKETCH.

IT was well, perhaps, to have seen first the withered cheeks of Pharaoh the Great. · The glamour of his fame and name eclipses much of the splendour of Egyptian kings, after and before. But when one has been told of, or seen face to face, a hero, great in peace as great in war, one naturally wishes to see the father who begat him, and to hear of the mother who gave him birth.

Let us turn and look on the features of the father of Rameses II., the man best known to us to-day by the name of Seti, or Sethos the First, and let us recall something of his life's history.

Variously named as this great king was—now Oimeneptah, now Osirimeneptah (from which by metathesis, the historian Diodorus got the distorted form Osymundyas), now Usiris, now Men-meri—we find his cartouche or seal signature quite as varied as the sounding of his name.

Sometimes, for the first letter of his name, a long-eared Abyssinian dog is seen to be carved. Sometimes the letter A, which this dog represented, has been chiselled out, and either a hawk has been carved in its place to signify the same letter, or else an Osiris is seen sitting, to signify that the royal name should begin with an O and not with an A.

But the latest Egyptologists speak of him as variously called Mineptah I., which means the favourite of Vulcan, or Seti I., which bespeaks his adherence to a connection, by descent or inclination, with the Baal worshippers and believers in Typhon, of the Phœnician or Mesopotamian country to the north.

At first sight it might seem of little matter that this king, the father of Rameses II. the Great, should bear this name. We will endeavour to show that there is much in the name, and that we may do this more clearly, we must give an account of the ending of the former dynasty, the eighteenth dynasty as it is called, which existed from 1700 to 1400 B.C., and of the troubles that fell upon the land preceding the nineteenth dynasty, of which Seti's father, Rameses I., was founder in the year 1400 B.C.

The Shepherd Kings, those strange people whose Tartar-looking faces remain to us on the black basalt sphinxes, Mariette Bey discovered in the field of Zoan, had reigned their 500 years, and had passed away. After a struggle of forty years' civil war, or war of independence, in which the brave Taa-Ken * had fallen for his country and the true kings of old; those rightful kings of old, the Pharaohs of the true line, ascended the throne, and Aahmes, or Amosis, the general and admiral in one, began the eighteenth dynasty of Thebes, in about the year 1700 B.C.

That eighteenth dynasty was glorious with such warriors as Thothmes III., such builders as Amenhotep III., whose mighty Memnon figures sit to-day above the Theban plain, memorials of marvellous engineering feats and royal thirst for glory.

But the end of that dynasty was troubled, and a foreign queen—Thi, or Tia, or Taia—was the cause of it.

Amenhotep loved not wisely, but too well; and from whatever land † his foreign consort had come, she brought with her such a profound horror for the worship of the sun's disk, as opposed to the orthodox worship of Amen Ra, the sun, at his rising, noon, and setting, and so instilled the new heresy into her son, Amenophis IV., that he, when he came to the throne

---

* Called also Tiu-aquen and Se-qenen-Ra. His body may be seen at the Gîzeh Museum, with the death-wound upon his forehead.

† It is now known that she was the daughter of Tushratta the king of Mitanni. Interesting correspondence-tablets between the king and the court of Babylon, Mesopotamia, and Phœnicia have been lately discovered at Tell el-Amarna.

H

in 1466 (?), threw off the faith of his fathers, the
worship of the sun as an embodiment of good and life.
He changed his name to Khu-en-aten, or Chut-en-aten
—that is, "the splendour of the sun's disk,"—turned his
back upon Memphis and Thebes, and set up a new
capital at a place in middle Egypt, on the eastern
bank of the Nile, 200 miles south of Cairo.   Here
rubbish mounds, with their broken sherds and
evidences of scattered ruins, spread behind a palm
grove by the river, over a narrow two miles of ground,
and are called to-day Tell el-Amarna, and there, in
the cliffs that form a natural amphitheatre to the plain,
he bade his architect, one Bek by name, to hew
magnificent temples and tomb-grottoes in hard stone
to Aten, the sun's disk.   He had fire altars cut out of
red syenitic granite, and portraits of himself carved,
burning incense to the disk of the sun, each ray of
which stretches out a hand towards the heretic king
to bless him.

  This heresy, with its insult to the sun-god Ra, its
obliteration of the sun-god's name from the public
monuments, and its desertion of the temples of
Ammon at Thebes, tore the land and divided it.
Khu-en-aten's young wife, Nofer Tai, or Nofer-i-Thi,
died in decline—a judgment from heaven, I expect
it was said, at the time, by the orthodox.

  The priestly caste rose against the king, and it is
not unlikely that the Horus, or Horemhib, who suc-

ceeded, as last king of the eighteenth dynasty, 1466 B.C. (?), was rather of the priestly, than of the royal line —a man brought from the darkness of comparative retirement to the " fierce light that beats upon a throne."

This Horus had been apparently much what Joseph had been in Egypt, a kind of provincial governor or ruler. Gentle and upright, it was said of him: " He took pleasure in justice, which he carried in his heart. He followed the gods Thoth and Ptah in all their ways, and they were his shield and protection on earth evermore." " Heaven and earth rejoice together," says a contemporary account of the accession of Horemhib to the throne. " Heaven kept festival, and all the land was glad; the deities rejoiced on high; the people of Egypt raised their rapturous songs of praise even unto Heaven; and great and small united their voices with one accord. It was as if Horus, son of Isis, were once more presenting himself after his triumph over Set."

He did what he could to mediate between the heretics of the sun-disk followers and the much-abused and ill-treated worshippers of the sun under the name Amen Ra. He restored the seat of government at Thebes, with its cult of the sun-god, and beautified and built up the town of Memphis, with its worship of Vulcan.

He died childless, after a reign of twenty-one years. It is believed that a generation of heretic kings succeeded; be that as it may, it is possible that the man who came to the throne as the establisher of the nineteenth dynasty, in about the year 1400 B.C., was Horemhib's brother (?) His name, Rameses I., betokens his fidelity to the old national form of worship.

He was a bold man, whoever he was, who dared at such a time, without a drop of royal blood in his veins, to assume the sovereignty of a land, troubled by the as yet unhealed division between the worshippers, and threatened with invasion from a power—the precursor in might of Nineveh and Babylon—that with its confederacy of 128 cities (whose names are preserved to us in the list of the victories of Thothmes III. at Karnak) was growing in the north under the title of the Khita, or Hittites.

But this protector of the Egyptian reformation, Rameses I., had, as is evidenced by the sculpture of his solemn coronation on the entrance gates of the Temple of Karnak, at any rate the goodwill of the priestly party at Thebes.

And though his reign was short, he went to war with the Hittites, and made, what was of the utmost moment for the safety of Egypt and the restoration of peace and commerce, an offensive and defensive alliance with Saplel or Saprer, the Hittite king.

We have all heard a good deal of Wady Halfa during this late Soudanese campaign. At Wady Halfa, then called Behani, in the second year of the warrior Rameses I.'s reign, the king built a stone house for the temple of his divine father Hor Khem—the sun, that is, as he rises and sets—and it was filled with men and maidens from the tribesmen that he conquered. The Soudanese, whom he led in bonds, were there set to minister to the honour of the god, whom Rameses, and nobody but Rameses the conqueror, dared to call " his divine father."

Short was the reign of Rameses I., but before he entered his eternal house—the rock chamber that is with us to this day, the oldest in the Valley of the Kings, at Thebes,—he had had the foreknowledge to realise that what the Egyptian nobles and the Egyptian priests cared for, next to peace from their enemies, was blue blood in the veins of their kings. And it is probable that he induced his son Seti to look to it that he should wed, if possible, a princess of the late royal line that ceased to be a ruling line when Horus, or Horemhib, died.

Now, there was a daughter of that beautiful queen, Taia, wife of Amenophis III. She it was, you remember, who brought the sun-disk worship into the land, from Mesopotamia. Royal blood on both sides was in this lady's veins, for Taia was a princess in her own right, of Naharaina, the land of the rivers to the north ; and on the monuments she is spoken of as " the marvel, the daughter of the chief of Naharaina— the great royal lady—Tii, the living one."

This princess's sister had married the heretic, Khu-en-Aten, and one would have thought that Seti I. would have never looked that way; but Seti was determined to bring back royalty into the ruling line. If he was a commoner, his son should be royal, or at least on his mother's side ; and as for the priestly caste, had he not shown, and had not his father, Rameses I., given proof, that Amen Ra, and not Aten —the sun and not its disk—was the object of his worship and his reverential care.

Tuäa, the princess whom Seti wooed, must have been very beautiful—not so sprightly and full of delicate vivacity as was her mother Taia, if we may judge by comparing the profiles of the mother and daughter that are preserved to us ; but the more Egyptian type of face was hers, and she bequeathed it, as we know, to Rameses the Great.

But how came it about that she, Tuäa, the daughter of Taia—whether Tartar or Chaldean, Assyrian or pre-Canaanite, we cannot say—should have looked on Seti with favour, and given him her heart and hand ?

We are in the land of conjecture, but this much is certain, Seti's very name shows that he was allied, by family tradition, with that strange race of shepherd kings, the Hyksos, who for about 400 years had possessed themselves of the Delta, and reigned at Zoan and Avaris.   They worshipped Set, or Sutek, the Typhonic spirit of war and might and evil, often, how-

ever, invoked as the beneficent god under the name
of Set-Nub, or the Golden Set, and it is very doubtful
whether, for all their hate against their false worship,
the Egyptians bore such animus against their shepherd kings personally, as Manetho would have us to
suppose.

Now, wherever these strange shepherd kings, who
knew Joseph and welcomed him to honour, came
from, and whether Chaldean or Assyrian, Turanian or
Semitic, in type of face, matters not.   This much is
certain, that Seti's family had tender leanings of
tradition, perhaps of blood, towards their memory ;
for we find on a celebrated stone tablet of syenitic
granite, found at Zoan by Mariette Bey, a picture of
Rameses the Great, Seti's son, offering wine to the
god Set, the old national deity of the shepherd kings,
and this in honour of his father Seti's memory. The
god is wearing the white crown, and holds the key of
life in his right hand, and in his left, the shepherd's
staff or crook of office.

This tablet is put up by a high officer of the court
of Rameses II., and he tells us : " His Majesty has
ordered it to be set up for the great name of his
father, for the sake of setting up the name of the father
of his father, from his parent Seti to the King Set,
Aahpeppeh, Nubti, or Apophis, 400 years before."

" Hail to thee, Set, son of Nut, Aahpeppeh, in the
boat of millions of years, overthrowing enemies before

the boat of the sun." So concludes the officer's prayer on this important "tablet of the 400 years."

Here is evidence, little expected, to make us guess that Seti I. was not Egyptian proper, but was, as his name implied, kin to the far-off shepherd kings. And herein was probably the secret of the willingness of Tuäa, daughter of Taia the Mesopotamian, to wed with Seti, and bring back royal blood to the throne of Thebes.

Hard by that tablet at Zoan, has been unearthed the Hyksos sphinx, with its name " *Suteck*, the beneficent god, the presiding deity," graven upon its head. And those who look upon that portrait of Apophis, the Pharaoh of Joseph's time, and then gaze upon the face of Tuäa and Seti I., the parents of Rameses II. the Pharaoh of the Exodus, will find it easy enough to see a marked similarity, in racial cast of countenance, to the Hyksos sphinx of Zoan, and a marked unlikeness to such Egyptian types as are found on the sphinxes of an earlier day.

For the Egyptian sphinx proper, with its head-dress of spreading hawk wings, wears always a smile upon its rounded face ; its eyes are wide apart and open wide. The sphinx of Zoan, the shepherd king sphinx, with the type of Seti and Rameses II.'s face upon it, has eyes nearer, chin more projecting, more strong, cheek-bones prominent, and a mouth that falls at the corners ; nor ever does it wear the wing-shaped wig, except where, as is the case in one instance, the Pharaoh Rameses has sculptured the flowing head-dress of the shepherd king into the wing-shaped wig of his own time.

I have said enough to show that there was probably a family tradition, as well as, perhaps, an under-current of religious feeling, that brought about the happy match between Seti I. and Tuäa, the princess.

The son born of that union was Pharaoh the Great, and the world has never forgotten, and never can forget, the issue of that wooing and that wedding.

Seti was likely at once to feel the power of having brought in royalty to rule with him. The people of the Delta, who had always remembered the beneficent rule of the shepherd kings, would be with him. They knew his name. The priests of the people at Thebes would be with him, for he cared for ancient This, near Abydos, where Osiris' head was buried, and took the name of Osirimenepthah; while it is clear that the crown name Meneptah, "Favourite of Vulcan the Creator," and his deeds of honour and restoration at Memphis, the home of that god, would win him hearts in that old white-walled city, by Sakkara's palms and pyramids.

The Israelites, who had fared well under the shepherd kings, possibly because of their common Chaldean origin, may have suffered somewhat under the kings of the eighteenth dynasty, but they do not appear to have been in any way molested by Seti and his Queen Tuäa, perhaps for a like reason. It was not till the great building period set in at Zoan, under Seti's son, Rameses the Great, that their lives were made bitter in the brickfields.

On the contrary, Seti I. seems at once to have felt that the land where the Hebrews dwelt, needed protection.

The Shashu, or Arabs, had, partly owing to the national dissensions of Egypt at the end of the eighteenth dynasty, and partly to Rameses I.'s weakish reign, partly to the long duration of peace and lack of hostile demonstrations between 1400 and 1366, determined to press up on to the eastern frontier of Egypt, and " find sustenance for themselves and cattle in the possessions of Pharaoh."

The Hebrews were no fighters ; the green fields of bersîm, clover, and lentils were laid waste, and a good deal of cattle-lifting went on.

Seti knew that successful war was one of the ways to establish himself in the hearts of his people, and with all the keen fighting blood of the vigorous north-eastern in his composition, and with his Queen Tuäa's goodwill, he determined to make a clean sweep of these Shashu, or Bedouins, from the Delta, and so win honour for Egypt, and gain the thanks of the Hebrew farmers into the bargain.

We have an elaborate picture-history of these wars

of Seti, preserved to us upon the outer wall at the
north side of the great hall at Karnak.

We shall speak of that great hall later on; it is
enough for us to know that six pictures, ranged in a
series, give us the principal events of this campaign
against the Bedouins. We can, by means of these,
trace the line of march from Etham to Migdol and
Baalzephon as far as Rehoboth, south of Beersheba,
and up Wady Arabah, as far as the hill frontiers of
Kanaan, somewhere near the Dead Sea.

The Bedouin country of Sinai and Edom, up to the
borders of Philistia or Zalu, was won and occupied.
The first victory at the fortress of Kanaan is thus
described :

"In the first year of King Seti—this is 1366 B.C.—
there took place, by the strong arm of Pharaoh, the
annihilation of the hostile Shashu from the fortresses
of Khetan, of the land of Zalu as far as Kanaan. . . . .
The king was against them as a fierce lion. They
were turned into a heap of corpses in their hill
country. They lay there in their blood. Not one
escaped to tell of his strength to the distant nations."

When I passed over the plain of El Kuwerah, east
of the Wady Arabah, and saw the bullets and cannon-
balls that told of the victory of Abbas Pasha against
the Bedouins of this century, I could not but, in heart,
go back to that far-off battle-day, more than 3200
years ago, when the Shashu lay there in their blood,

and think of the curse of every man's hand against the wandering Arabs, that had lain heavy upon these children of the desert all down the pitiless centuries.

The Bedouins, discomfited and decimated, were still not disheartened.   They made a stand in the land of the Kharu, or Phœnicians ; but Seti, in his chariot of war, whose pair of horses was called "Ammon gives him Strength," dashed into their ranks and utterly routed them.

From Jamnia's bloody field King Seti went to the interior, and overthrew the villages of the North Syrians, known by the name of the Rutennu, fair-faced men with blue eyes and red pointed beards, who wore thick under-garments, and sleeves to their coats, showing us that they were, by origin, dwellers in a colder country than the Rutennu of their own day.

The battle-picture shows us, in this first year of Seti's reign, a little boy fighting in the war-chariot at his father's side.   That little boy grew up to be Rameses II. the Great, the warrior monarch of the sixty-seven years of wondrous history. He learned stern business in war early, and there was a reason in his early education.   Seti had determined that the son of his loins, who should bring back royal blood to the throne, should also bring to the throne a heart that delighted to "wash itself in the blood of his enemies." Like father like son. And here, in the Rutennu campaign, we read of how, "borne through the land by his

pair of horses, named ' Big with Victory,' Seti's joy is to undertake the battle, his delight is to dash into it."
" His heart is only satisfied at sight of the stream of blood, when he strikes off the heads of his enemies—a moment of the struggle of men is dearer to him than a day of pleasure." This is all of a piece with Seti's non-Egyptian parentage. The Egyptian proper was not cruel or bloodthirsty. One feels in the presence, rather, of men of the Assyrian type of character, monsters of Nineveh and bulls of Babylon, as one reads.

Another war-picture changes the scene. Seti has made a swift attack on Kadesh, the key of the North. " His war-chariot surprises the herdsmen in the fields ; his arms are very sharp." They slay the warriors as they sally from their citadel, and Kadesh is won.

There—where in later times the little Rameses, grown to be the Great, won such glory by his facing fearful odds in the single-handed battle, when " even his captains had deserted him, and he was all alone, and none other were with him "—there was an assault and sally, repulse and victory. But Seti's campaign was not at an end. Away north of this Kadesh, by the Orontes stream, lay the powers that were the fore-runners of Nineveh and Babylon, called in that day " The Great People." Two distinct races of men their monuments show them to have been, if we may trust their dress and manner of arms. They were the

Khitan Hittites. Mauthanar, the Khitan king, who had made a treaty, had broken it, and against the well-ordered hosts of the beardless, red-skinned men of Khita, Seti advanced.

"These are the miserable Hittites ; the king has proposed for them a great overthrow," says the inscription in the hall of Karnak ; and then the psalm of triumph bursts forth, and Seti is described as " like to a jackal leaping through the land, a grim lion in ambush, a powerful bull with a pair of sharpened horns."

It is pretty clear that, after the battle, peace on honourable terms was concluded. " His war-cry was like to the war-cry of Baal Sutek" (a hint here of Seti's Hyksos descent) ; but " the enmity of all peoples was turned to friendship," and so King Seti set his face to the South.

When I stood, a few years since, beneath the last remnants of the ancient grove of Lebanon, I seemed to hear, not only the axes of Tyre and Sidon ring out for Solomon's Temple, but also the axes of the men of Zor, whom Seti had conquered, merrily chopping away at the goodly cedar trees for Seti I. and his triumphant army, and I knew how, on the Karnak temple-walls, was a picture of the men of Kanaan and the mountaineers of Lebanon at work at the highest and straightest trees, and that an inscription, Brugsch Bey has restored, described the scene :

"The inhabitants of Limanun fell the trees for a great ship on the river in Thebes of the South, and in like manner for King Seti's high masts at Amon's temple in Thebes."

It was a glorious return the conqueror accomplished. Priests and nobles met him at the border fortress-city of Etham, and gave King Seti goodly welcome home. "Thou hast triumphed over thine enemies," they sang; "may thy life as king, be long as the sun of heaven."

All questions of royal right divine were now set at rest. The little Rameses, Seti's son, was ever, in future, at his father's side ; and though not yet associated with him on the throne, he goes again with his father Seti to the war. This time the enemy are the light-skinned, fair-headed peoples who dwell by the Mediterranean Sea—the Marmoridæ, the Greeks, and Lydians, and the Libyans to the west, who wore the double ostrich plume and the side locks of hair.

On the north wall of Karnak, Seti is seen in his chariot, whereof the horses were called " Victorious is Amon." Seti has pierced one of the " Thuhennu " warriors with an arrow, of a cloth-yard long, and, changing his bow to his left hand, he has lifted his battle-axe to cleave his enemy to the chin. Ten of the foe have fallen beneath the hoofs of prancing and plume-headed horses. The inscription tells us, " he utterly destroyed them as they stood upon the battle-field.

They could not hold their bows, and remained hidden in their caves for fear of the king."

A second return home in triumph is celebrated. The Temple of Amon in Thebes has its coffers filled with all manner of spoil—exquisite golden drinking-cups, with handles in shape of animal heads, telling us of the artistic handicraft of the jewellers of those old days, thirty-two centuries and a half ago ; but though the songs of the priests of the Temple of Amon are in our ears—before the great Seti, saying, " Hail to thee, King of Egypt ! Happy is the people subject to thy will. But he who o'ersteppeth thy boundaries shall appear led as a prisoner in chains "—we cannot help noting how, though the dedication of all this spoil to Amon and his wife Nut, and their young son, Khonsu, or the Moon, went gloriously forward with aid of sistrum and harp, the central figure of all that joy, was the little son and heir, "the pillar of a people's hope," the idol of his mother Tuäa, the queen.

In a small Nubian temple there is a sculpture of Queen Tuäa, receiving her well-beloved darling, on his return from his second campaign ; and it is not out of place here to observe that, as we learn from the great historical inscription of Abydos, there was a parental pride in the boy which, apart from political considerations, made Seti care for the lad's companionship.

"I desire," said Seti, " to behold his grandeur while I am yet alive. I will have him crowned as king. Place the regal circlet on his brow."

"Thus spake he," wrote, in after-time, Rameses, "with good intention in his very great love of me. Still he left me in the court of the women, and chose me attendant maidens who wore a harness of leather."

Whether the actual crowning of Rameses, the son, took place at this return from the Libyan campaign in triumph, we know not ; but it is certain that from that time forward, while the boy still wore the youth's lock of hair, he seems to have been, in the eyes of all the people, a central figure on public occasions, a kind of co-regent with his father, the darling of his mother, and chief delight of Seti the king.

But not only were success in war, and the re-establishment of the temples in Thebes, and the setting up of cedar masts upon the propylons, necessary to insure to Seti that which his soul desired—namely, the full establishment of his kingship in the hearts of peasants and people ; Mammon, as well as Ammon, was to be cared for ; temples and public works needed gold for the wages of the workmen ; and now in the ninth year of his reign, we learn from a sandstone tablet on the walls of a rock-temple at Wady Alaki, how that " the king's heart wished to see the mines from whence the gold is brought," and how, on the 20th

I

day of October, Seti undertook an expedition, by the old merchants' road, from Coptos through the desert called "the land of the gods," east of the Nile, opposite Edfû, towards Berenice, to visit and inspect the gold mines, and see what could be done to supply a waterless road, with wells for caravans, and the gold-washers, with means of prosecuting their industry.

The inscription tells us "that Seti made a halt, and determined to wipe out reproach from the place where aforetime men cried out, overtaken with thirst, 'Land of perdition!'"

"He had the well bored for them. Thus did King Seti do a good work—the beneficent dispenser of water, who prolongs life for his people."

"The difficult road is opened up. The gold can now be carried up. May the king flourish like Horus, because he has founded a memorial in the land of the gods—the desert; because he has bored for water in the mountains."

Ani, the king's son, of Kush, the chief architect, has left no record to tell us of the success of the gold mining and waterworks undertaking; but we read how "the water flowed from the rock in great abundance, like the waters of the Nile at Abu," and we also hear how the king Seti ascribed his success to Heaven, and said :

"The god has heard my prayer. The water has come forth in abundance, the road that had no water has been made good under my rule. The shepherds shall have pasture for their flocks."

Nor was it only those shepherds in the desert of Redesieh for whom Seti had a father's care. He appears to have had a hand in carrying out the building of a great wall, like the wall of the Romans across our own England, which should stretch from Heliopolis, the City of the Sun, where Moses grew up to manhood, right to Pelusium, the Port Said of to-day, for the better protection of the shepherds in the plain, from Asiatic or Arab invasion.

One can never enter the Porta de Popolo of Rome, or stand at Trinita da Monti, without remembering that the obelisks that stand there, were set up at the City of the Sun, to the honour of the wall-builder who cared for the herdsmen of the Delta.

And Seti evidently was an agriculturist and a believer in commerce. He determined to bring sweet water and find a water-way for the farm produce of his people, and he constructed, it is believed, the first great canal that joined the Nile to the Red Sea.*

We have seen the father of Pharaoh the Great now in his capacity of warrior and of gold-digger.

---

* A picture of this canal is preserved to us on the exterior north wall of Karnak. Seti I. is represented in his chariot, driving three strings of prisoners of war before him, and just about to cross it. (See Ebers's "Egypt Illustrated," pt. ii. p. 21.)

It remains for us to note his pre-eminence as temple and tomb-builder.

It must be understood that the temples were of two kinds : partly memorial temples, which should embalm, as it were, the memory of the great dead ; these were, for the most part, built on the western side of the river, for the sun sank in the west, and the great dead had gone down the dark way after him. Partly temples that were raised as acts of piety to the gods—Ammon, the male god; Mout or Mut, the woman god ; and Khons, the son.

Sometimes the memorial temple, as in the case of the Memnonium of Seti at Kûrnah, embraced both ends.

It should be borne in mind that the temples to the gods, the great national sanctuaries, were not meant for congregational use or public services. They were huge secret hiding-places of the treasure dedicated to the god, and retired Holies of Holies, wherein the god himself should rest, and be approached with honour by his children on earth, the kings and queens of the reigning dynasty. The people seldom saw beyond the outer gate. The priests seldom issued from it, except to go backward and forward to their houses, or to take part in some national thanksgiving or royal burial.

But since secrecy for treasure and sanctity for the god, were needed, these huge temple prisons were

surrounded with wall after wall, so arranged as not to
prevent the line or "dromos" of sphinxes, and obelisks,
and colossi running directly from outside, right
through all the courts, beneath the vast towered gates
in the various enclosing walls, up to the sanctuary.

It is true that the priestly ritual, quite apart from
congregational purposes, needed ample space for its
processions, and we find that most of the temples
were so arranged as to admit of there being endless
corridors and pillared courtyards, open to the sun
or closed from its rays.

Approaching by the sphinx avenue, and entering
through a thirty-five feet "vallum" of mud-brick, one
passed beneath the pylons, or tower gates, perhaps as
much as 120 feet high, as at Edfû, with their cedar
masts on either side, to an inner ward, beneath other
gates less high; thence into the peristyle court, a
court where the people were perhaps allowed to
gather at times, where the priests took air and
exercise. Thence we should have entered between
two great obelisks, or colossi, into the really important
hall for religious service, called the hypostyle hall,
shut in from the sun by great slabs of stone, gilt with
stars, and painted or enamelled blue, resting upon
stone beams, and these in turn upon a forest of pillars;
the light arranged for, by the lifting up of a central
portion of the roof, and admitting thus of clerestory
windows.

Beyond this hall of columns, when we had got used to the comparative dusk, we should have seen the sanctuary, where the god, in a separate sanctum, in a monolithic shrine, dwelt in darkness and mystery; and round that little shrine were gathered retiring-rooms for the priests and artificers who attended to the sacrifices, dressing-rooms, store-chambers, side-chapels, &c.; and beneath, in vast crypts and vaults, lay concealed the temple treasures. A huge bath or tank within the temple area, called the "Sacred Lake of the Sun"—for the purposes of ritual when the golden bark of the sun was launched upon it—completed the temple furnishing.

But what must have struck one most, if one had entered the temple enclosure, was the fact that from floor to roof of the hypostyle, or the hall of columns, from ground to cornice of the peristyle colonnade, or courtyard walls, from base to summit of the towering pylons, colour and rich engraved sculpture, in low relief and deep incised beauty of decoration, occupied all the available space. Differing evidently in age and worth of execution, but constantly repeating the same motive of ornament, the same pictures of battle and leading of captives in triumph, and the same pictures of offering by the king, at the shrine of the god or goddess, costly oblations, with prayer for good luck.

The fact is, that each king in each dynasty had a hand in adding, court by court, to the shrine of the

national deities ; each vying in splendour of decoration or size in building,

And since the whole act of building these halls to the
god, was an act of sacrifice or adoration, it was fitting
that each victory, or each deed of prowess, by which
the king had obtained honour and glory, should be
depicted, not only as a memorial of proud honour, but
as an act of dedication—a public declaration that all
these things came by the will of the god, and were a
public acknowledgment of hearty thanks for heavenly
favours.

Seti I. may have had within him something of the
power to build, that actuated the later men of Babylon
and Nineveh. His Hyksos blood, if it had the
Assyrian life within it, cared much to make the might
of his name be known by the might of his hands, as
architect. He added "splendid buildings" to the
temples at Memphis and Heliopolis, but the buildings
that remain to us, most notably his, are the temple of
Osiris in the desert of Abydos ; the Memnonium of
Seti at old Gurnah, or Kûrnah, on the western side of
the river at Thebes ; the great hall of columns at
Api, or as it is better known, Karnak, on the eastern
bank of the Nile at Thebes, just opposite ; and the
beautiful tomb he wrought for himself in the Valley of
the Kings, known to-day as Belzoni's tomb.

Let us visit them all, omitting, as being of less importance, one minor temple we had almost forgotten

to mention, a temple to Seckhet Bast, or Pasht, the cat-headed or lion-headed goddess of force and passion, away at Beni Hasân.

At Abydos, Seti determined to put himself beyond the reproaches of heresy which his name Set might imply, by raising a temple to Osiris, somewhere near the mound where fable had it, that the head of the just and light-giving Osiris had been found, after Typhon, the spirit of darkness and of evil, had hewed his body in pieces, and it had been discovered and buried by Isis, his queen.

The Egyptian's hope of immortality, and his faith in the power of good over evil, of the ultimate triumph of the spirit over the material, was symbolised by this myth of Osiris, Isis, and Horus ; though, as for the tales of these legends being, as some aver, on a parallel with, or even a prefiguring of, the death and resurrection of Jesus Christ, there is very little truth in them. But to the Egyptian the fight of light and right against darkness and wrong, was a constantly recurring thought, a faith re-born with every rising sun ; and so by the mound of Kom es Sultân, where the pious Egyptian and orthodox believers were buried, century after century, in hope of a joyous resurrection, Seti determined to raise a temple to Osiris the good.

It was an age of transition in architecture. Seti had his own views about it, and not content with the terraced temples after the fashion of Hātshepset at Dêr-

el-Bahari, or the great colonnades of Ameuoph III. at
Luxor, he built here at Abydos a small temple, with a
sevenfold avenue of columns and portals ending in
seven chapels, whose roofs, walls, and pillars remain
to us to-day—the wonder of colour-artists and workers
in stone. There is nothing better in Egyptian art of
the middle empire, nothing more finished is found in
the whole Theban range of art, than the decorations of
the temple to Osiris and Isis, Horus, Ammon, Harmachis, Ptah, and Seti I. at Abydos; we know the name
of its architect, " Hi," and we realise that here, art of
wall-chiselling was at its best. Sakkarah and the
tombs of Tih and Ptahhotep are not able to show
finer work. The temple is interesting as containing
on the north wall of the inner court, a figure of Seti
offering a little statue of the goddess of truth to
the seated Osiris: this picture is so famous I will
describe it. Seti is seen in full profile, wearing the
pshent, or royal head-dress, with the Uræus basilisk upon it, and streamers falling from it behind;
he is beardless, and without any hair upon his face.
A six-banded necklace is on his neck, a triple bracelet
on each of his upper arms, and a double bracelet on
each of his wrists; the face is full of refinement—
almost feminine in beauty; both hands are noticeable
for length of fingers and for their tapering delicacy.

His left hand is raised in attitude of supplication;
his right hand, though the draughtsman has twisted

it quite round, so that the thumb is towards the spectator, holds a little sacrificial bowl, and in the bowl is seated a miniature image of the goddess of truth and justice, " Ma " by name.

I wonder if children in England, when they cry to their mothers, know that they are addressing Truth and Justice twice over, and speaking the best Egyptian possible ?

She—the goddess " Ma "—is kneeling in attitude of a suppliant, and one knee is raised ; upon this she rests her right hand, holding the " anch," or crux ansata— the key of life.   On her head she wears the ostrich plume, the symbol of law.   The whole idea of the little figure, " Ma " being thus offered by the suppliant King Seti to the judge of the great under-world, probably centres in the thought that the king is professing himself a law-abiding spirit and truthful man, and would have the goddess of truth and justice to act as mediator between himself and his judge ; and we know, from the sarcophagus of Seti, how constantly Seti is spoken of as " the truthful one."   We expect he was a king of his word.

Another celebrated picture represents Seti and his son Rameses the Great taming a bull ; and in the corridor close by, was discovered by Dümichen in 1864, that history-making tablet, known to us as " the tablet of Abydos," which contained the names of seventy-six kings, the predecessors of Seti's royal ancestors right

back to the half-mythical first Egyptian monarch, the
founder of the empire—Menes. There were more
than seventy-six monarchs, but the artist used an
artist's liberty, and gives us only the names of those
kings considered to be the ever-living ones, the kings
of deathless fame. The list is specially valuable as
giving us the names of the kings, with one or two
exceptions, quite unaltered, and the order of the kings
in strict historical sequence, so far as the monuments
have allowed us verification.

On this important stone-document the young
Rameses is seen, standing by his father—for Seti always
took care, as has been before said, to associate his
son in public work with him, for a very good reason—
offering homage to these great royal ancestors.

When I tell you that it is, thanks to that tablet of
Abydos, that we can get approximately at the dates of
Hebrew history in Holy Writ ; thanks to that, that we
can learn that Seti Meneptah, Rameses the First's
son, who came to the throne in 1366, was the second
king of the nineteenth Theban dynasty, we realise its
worth as *bonâ fide* historic authority, after it has stood
the test of three thousand two hundred centuries and
a half.*

On the wall opposite this tablet of Abydos, Rameses,

---

* A picture of this tablet is given us in Ebers's "Egypt
Illustrated," part ii. p. 212.

Seti's son, is seen, under his father's direction, pouring libations over a vase of flowers, in honour of the deities whose names are there inscribed. On the left of the entrance, on the wall to the south of the central door, is another notable inscription, telling of how it came to pass that Rameses, the son of Seti, finished the temple building.

As we leave the halls of Abydos, we can picture to ourselves the funeral procession that somewhere about the year 1333 B.C. came sadly here, across the rich plain from the Nile, to leave the great builder Seti— the swathed and silent mummy we have so lately unwrapped—for a time within its walls, before it entered its eternal house in the Valley of Kingly Sleep, at Thebes.

Yes, and in the next year following, another procession is seen approaching the unfinished temple of Abydos, by way of the sacred canal of Nifur.

A magnificent festival has just been celebrated at Thebes in honour of Amen Ra, and Rameses, "whose heart," so the Abydos inscription tells us, "had a tender feeling towards his parents, has, on a bright September morning, started to return home." As the ships sailed on, "they threw their brightness on the river," and now they turn aside, and the canal banks are gay with the multitude, but the king "is sad." For Abydos is reached; the columns are not raised; the statues lie in the sand. The priests have appro-

priated the revenue, and the graves of the dead are
forlorn.   The chamberlains are called.   "Their
noses," we read, "touched the ground"; and after
they have filled the air with flattery, the King, Rameses,
speaks :

"The most beautiful thing to behold, the best
thing to hear, is a child with a thankful breast, whose
heart beats for his father."   He then gives a history
of his early up-bringing and his father Seti's tender
kindness, and adds : " I will renew the memorial and
clothe the walls of my parent."   The chamberlains
answer: " Do good even as thou willest.   Let thy
heart be satisfied in doing what is right.   The gods
will honour, hereafter in heaven, him who will honour
them on earth."

Then the king commanded, and gave commission
to the architects.   I expect " Hi " was called, and the
great court painter " Amen-uah-su."

And we read : " He superintends the people of the
masons and of the stone-cutters, with the help of the
graver, and the draughtsmen, and all kinds of artists,
to build the holy place for his father, and to raise up
what had fallen into decay in the temple of his father,
who sojourns among the deceased ones."

I do not know, in Egyptian records, any more touching prayer than that of Rameses II. to his father, the
Osiris-king, Seti, as recorded at Abydos :

" Awake, raise thy face to heaven, behold the sun,

my father Meneptah, thou who art like god. Thou restest in the deep like Osiris, while I rule, like Ra, among men. Thou hast entered the realm of heaven, thou art joined to the sun and the moon. When the sun rises, thine eyes behold his splendour, when it sinks on the earth, thou art in its train. But I obtain by prayer the breath of life at thy awaking, thou glorious one. I praise thy numberless names day by day—I, who love my father, I will be guided by thy virtue. Come, speak to the great sun-god Ra, for me, that he may grant me length of days. My heart beats for thee, and so long as I live, I will be safeguard of the honour of thy name."

Seti, in answer to this prayer, so the inscription records, appeared, and promised health, wealth, and joy to his loving son, and in addition, that which Rameses most desired, length and abundance of days. We know that promise was literally fulfilled : God, not Seti, granted the mighty Pharaoh nearly 100 years and a reign of 67 summers. Let us go from Abydos to Thebes.

Seti seems ever to have had before him the fact that life was not for ever here beneath the sun, and that the memory of man soon fades. And it speaks well for his filial piety that he should have builded, to perpetuate his father's memory, a cenotaph which, though it is but ill preserved, allows us to know that it comprised a hall behind a ten-columned portico, eight of

which columns still stand, and was approached
through an avenue of 250 feet, between a double row
of sphinxes. This building, called to-day the Memnonium of Seti,* was called in Seti's time " the splendid
temple-building of King Meneptah Seti in the city
of Amon, on the western side by Thebes, in sight of
Api," as Karnak was called.

It was dedicated to Rameses I., Seti's father, and
to the gods Osiris, Horus, and Ammon. And there
is a pathetic inscription, which tells us how that Seti's
son, Rameses II., or Pharaoh the Great, " finished the
house of his father, King Meneptah Seti, for he (Seti)
died and entered the realm of heaven, and he united
himself with the sun-god in heaven when this house
was being built. The gates showed a vacant space,
and all the walls of stone and brick were yet to be
raised; all the work in it of writing—that is, hieroglyphics—and painting was unfinished."

What Rameses did for Abydos and his father's
memory, so did he here, and in memory of his grandfather and to the glory of his father Seti, did that
well-beloved and well-loving son show forth the true
gratitude of a child who honoured his " fore-elders."

It speaks volumes for Seti, that Rameses the Great,
" the child whose heart was full of thanks towards his
father that raised him up," should do this. Well had

---

* The Temple of Kûrnah.

the young king said: "I will not neglect my father's tomb as children do. Men shall speak of me as a faithful son, and shall estimate the strength of my father, in me his child."

But Api,* or Karnak, with its dower of twenty-five centuries of national worship, its architects' endeavours under twenty monarchs and nine dynasties ; Karnak, made glorious by kings from the end of the Old empire of Egypt, 2466 B.C., to the end of the New, 332 B.C., with memorials from Usertsen I. to Cæsar Augustus ; Karnak, a collection of eleven temples on ground, nearly half a mile long and 2000 feet wide, on the eastern side of the river at Thebes ; Karnak—whose founder was Amenemhat I., the first king of the twelfth Theban dynasty, about 2466 B.C.—saw the greatest of Seti's works. Usertsen I., so Manetho tells us, was he who founded it, but from inscriptions discovered, an earlier king had commenced to build there. Karnak had in Seti's time seen the vicissitudes of 1100 years, and for 500 years of that time, during the Hyksos kings' reign, had probably remained but little cared for. But Thothmes III., of the eighteenth dynasty, 1600 B.C., had reared its doors and towers ;

---

* The civil name of Thebes was Api, or Apiu—*i.e.*, the City of Thrones : with the article *t* or *ta* prefixed, it became Ta-Apiu ; hence, by corruption, Thebes. Its sacred name was Nu—*i.e.*, the City ; or Nu-amen—*i.e.*, the City of Amen, the No or No-amon of Scripture.

his son Amenhotep II., 1566 B.C., had inscribed
its walls and southern gate. Now, in the nineteenth
dynasty, the priests of Ammon had enriched its portals
with the pictorial scene of Rameses I.'s coronation,
1400 B.C. And Seti, Rameses' son, would add a
further glory, and eclipse all builders that had gone
before. So he set himself to rear a stupendous hypostyle hall, wherein the priests of Ammon might perform
their processional acts of worship, and wherein the
history of his own wars might be, by the help of Hi
and Amen-uah-su, pictured forth, as we have in the
first part of this chapter described.

That hall of columns is the largest in all Egypt:
340 by 170 feet (325 by 160 feet, according to Brehm
and Dümichen), in length and breadth, and in the
centre, 80 feet in height, are figures that give us little
idea of its size ; but when one adds that the whole of
Notre Dame at Paris, could stand on the ground occupied by this one hall, and that it is ten times the size
of the white hall in the palace at Berlin, one gets a
better notion of its greatness.

The roof of this hall was made of stone slabs, each
of thirty tons weight, and these were placed on stone
beams which rested in turn upon 134 columns, and
weighed each of them forty-one tons. These gigantic
columns, coloured as they once were, from base to
capital, are partly papyriform, and partly in shape of
a budding lotus. Twelve of the columns that form the

K

central avenue of the halls have a height of 65 feet, a diameter of 11 feet, a circumference of 33 feet, and a hundred men could stand together on the enormous surface of each bud- or bell-shaped capital.

It was indeed a forest of stone, in which should grow, for eternity, the wonder of the world.

The worshipper who passed from out this forest gloom into the spacious open fore-court beyond, with its side colonnades, and stood beside the pylon by the great ramhead-sphinx avenue toward the Nile, now, at last, being uncovered for the gaze of Nile travellers, and in the direct line with the inside gate of Hāt-Shepset's temple, opposite, across the plain, must have felt that Seti I. was as a god, and his son Rameses, whose artists were working away to finish the sculptured pictures, was honouring a god, as he honoured his father. But, great as was the task to hew and set up that hall of columns, I think the task of the decorator strikes one to-day as being even more daring.

Seti died, it is not known when, for Rameses I. had been some time upon the throne, and virtual king before his father's death. His soul flew up, as old Egyptians would say, to join itself to the sun, and entered the golden boat of Ra to sail through Amenti the Vast.

But he must have parted with life sadly, for neither was the hall of columns complete, nor was the

memorial temple to his father at Karnak, nor the
elaborate shrine at Abydos, finished.   But his deepest
pain must have been that his own tomb, the house of
eternity fashioned for himself in the western cliff, was
not yet ready to receive his body.

He must have known that his mummied form would
needs have to rest in the salt and well-preserving sands
of Abydos for a time, before it would be sealed within
the splendid white sarcophagus, and laid beyond the
hands of time in that remarkable vault that he had
been hewing for it in the Valley of the Kings.

That tomb of Seti, Pharaoh's father, is worth de-
scribing.   It is for size, variety of colouring, and
abundance of pictorial wealth and inscription, unique.
The roof pictures of the golden chamber, the astrono-
mical teaching of its mythologies, are as wonderful as
is the substance of the text of the Book of Being in the
Underworld, discovered on the four walls of one of the
side chambers, called the " Chamber of the Law," which
describes, after Egyptian belief, the destruction of
mankind from off the face of the earth for its corruption and wickedness.

This tomb-chamber of Usiris, as Seti is called, is
seen to-day, a black speck at the foot of one of the
parched yellow *débris* mounds that have fallen from
the terraced limestone cliff above, in Bibân-el-Mulûk.

It is known as Belzoni's tomb, and had escaped the
quest of Greeks, and Romans, and Arabs, till a few

years ago, when Belzoni entered the hillside with his
torch, passed down a staircase of twenty-nine feet,
through a passage of eighteen feet, descried a second
stair of twenty-six feet, passed through a second
passage of twenty-nine feet, and found himself in a
small ante-chamber leading to a grand hall of twenty-
six feet square, upheld by four pillars.

Belzoni went on through a second hall, through
a passage and a second ante-room, and entered the
third and largest hall; thence he entered a small
room, and found—what? The body of Seti? No;
but the glorious white alabaster or arragonite sarcophagus wherein the king's body had once lain, and
which is now in the Soane Museum, Lincoln's Inn
Fields. All round and about were stowed wooden
images of Osiris, placed there by the men who made
lamentation for Seti, in the fourteenth century before
Christ, perhaps as media for the embodiment of the
souls who would be tilling his fields in Amenti the
Vast, or who should wait upon him when his body
rose, at the end of his 3000 years, to lay aside the
swathing-bands of eternity.

The 3000 years had passed, and Seti had risen—at
any rate, no Pharaoh was there; and back Belzoni
came, disappointed, but yet well satisfied, for here in
this wonderful tomb-chamber, or series of chambers,
planned by Seti himself, was such a marvel of wall
cutting and pictorial myth, as would unseal Egyptian

life and faith, and make the dead old centuries arise
from their silence and their sleep, and speak aloud.

As one enters Belzoni's tomb to-day, and proceeds
down its long stair-broken incline, to a depth of 150
feet and a length of 500 into the hot limestone, one
sees numberless side chambers cut neatly out of the
solid rock. In one of them the story of the Fall, or
rather of the Curse, is plainly written. Edouard
Naville has translated it, and I will transcribe a passage
or two :

" The god being by himself, after he has been established as king of men and the gods together, there
was silence. His majesty said : ' I call the gods
before me who were with me when I still was in the
divinity of the great deep Nun.' When the gods came
they bowed down before his majesty, and said, ' Speak
to us, that we may hear it.' Then said the sun-god to
Nun, the deity of the great deep : ' Thou firstborn of
the gods, whose issue I am, and you ancient gods,
behold the men who are born of myself ; they utter
words against me. I have waited, and have not destroyed them, till I shall have heard what you have to
say.'

" Then said the gods in the presence of his majesty :
' May thy grace allow us to go, and we shall smite them
who plot evil things, thy enemies, and let none remain
among them.' "

There is, within this wondrous tale of the destruction of mankind because of man's wickedness, something that links us on to the far past, which heard how the great deep swallowed up the world when it was lying in wickedness, a rebel against God, that so a new era and a new race of men might begin the mystery of godliness, and good living, and faithfulness once again.   There is a terrible trumpet-sound of just judgment from heaven for the sin of man.   But is there not also in it a note of aspiration sounding from the tomb of Usiris the justified, that bids us believe in a new heaven and a new earth, wherein dwelleth righteousness.   I cannot believe that that mythological record of the destruction of mankind was a mere fanciful invention.   It had its seat surely in the heart-stricken condition of a world that waited for the dawn.

Another scene is depicted, in which Āpepi, the serpent of evil, is dragged up from the depth of the sea, and slain by the god of light; and as one sees it one goes back in thought to our Scandinavian forefathers, and remembers how they too believed in the Midgard-worm at the bottom of the sea, and how Thor went out to catch it and Loki hindered him. Some common connection of idea binds the Vikings of olden times, with their belief in the worm of evil, to the sculptures of Seti's tomb.

We turn from the marvel of the tomb of Seti, leave the lizard in the hot sand and the bat in the darkness of its inner chambers; we leave the scarab upon his disk upon the wall guarded by his god ; we leave the designs on the stucco, at first sketched in in red, and altered after in good black paint by the master draughtsman ; and hie back in thought from the Valley of the Kings, to the little room of Sir John Soane, nigh filled by the great alabaster, arragonite sarcophagus in which once lay Seti the king, and which Belzoni in 1819 discovered—but, alas ! empty.

The figures and hieroglyphics which ornament the sarcophagus were engraved and then filled in with blue paint, and after many years of patient work the whole has been studied and carefully translated by M. Lefébure, and appears in the " Records of the Past," vol. x. and vol. xii.

The principal subject of the inscriptions on the sarcophagus, is the navigation of the sun nightly in the infernal regions. Twelve gates enclose successively twelve sections of space, and these gates correspond to the hours of night. Serpents with various names—Saa-set, Akebi, T'ebbi, Tek-her, Set-m-ar-f, Akheu-ar, Set-her, Ab-ta, Stu, Am-netu-f—guard the doors ; the first door has no serpent guardian, the last, or twelfth door has two—Sebi and Reri by name.

The god passes through the sections of space from gate to gate, having at his right hand the blessed, at his left the damned, who are represented in Egyptian perspective above and below.

The writings that accompany the illustrations are simply an edition, of Seti's time, of the Book of Hades. To put the subject-matter briefly : the sun, and the gods and the souls that accompany him, are swallowed up by the earth in the west, and rise in the east.

The underworld in Seti's tomb was looked at as having moral, as well as physical teaching. Apap, the symbol of evil, was punished in that underworld, and in that underworld dwelt good and bad; in that underworld the judgment throne was set and the books opened. Ra, the sun-god, rewarded the good, and Tum and Horus punished the evil-doers.

To give an idea of the amount of writing on the sarcophagus, I need only add that its translation occupies fifty pages of close octavo.

Amongst the subjects that appear which are familiar to Egyptologists, is the conquest of the great serpent, the Midgard-worm of Norse mythology—the great enemy of the human race, and a procession of its conquerors may be observed, carrying along its lengthy folds in solemn procession. There also may be seen that well-known judgment scene, in the hall of Osiris, Osiris on the throne, and Cerberus at the door, Thoth with the ibis-head, the Scales, Anubis and Horus of the hawk-head, to superintend the weighing of the heart, and the goddesses wearing the emblem of law and truth, the feathers on their heads, introducing the trembling and reverential soul who lifts his hands in attitude of prayer.

The cover of the sarcophagus, though broken, is engraved on its upper and outer side. The bottom of the sarcophagus, which is intact, shows us the goddess Nu, the goddess of the clear blue sky, her arms hanging down, her body wrapped about by folded wings, and over her head are inscribed her many names, the last of which is studded with stars, and signifies heaven.

The king, Seti-Meneptah the Truthful, speaks to Nu, and asks " to have his weakness put away from him, from what makes him weak "; in other words, prays to be delivered from the body of this death, and to have everlasting life.

And the answer comes from Seb, saying : " To this chosen one have I given purity on earth, and power in heaven." And, addressing Seti, he adds : "Seti-Merempthah the Truthful, thy mother Nu has given thee health which is in her for safety. Thou art in her arms ; thou shalt never die. Removed are evils which remained for thee. Horus stands beside thee ; thy mother Nu is come to thee ; she purifies thee ; she renews thee as a god, vivified, established among the gods."

Nu, the Very Great, answers : " I have made him a soul. His soul shall live for ever."

The chapter ends with the prayer of Seti, repeated,

asking to be delivered from the bonds of weakness, and from all that in his mortal life, or by reason of sin, made it exist.

A second chapter tells us how, in the presence of the Lord of Justice, freed from iniquity, and living for ever and ever for the double period of eternity, by the mouth, as it would seem, of Osiris, the Osiris-king ; son of Ra—Master of Diadems, Seti-Merempthah the Truthful—prayed for deliverance from all evil. His memory goes back to Egypt ; he sees his temples at Abydos and Karnak and Kûrnah filled with all manner of store, corn and barley in untold quantity, festivals being celebrated by the son of his body, funeral offerings, incense, oil, and all good and pure things upon which gods feed ; and he feels joyous-hearted, now united to life for ever, in the plains of offerings. But there is one touchingly pathetic note struck in his prayer ; it is this : " May the impious not take possession of me." The prayer heard and answered for the 3000 years has ceased to be of avail.

In June 1881, by the greed for backsheesh of a jackal-hunter, one of the Abd er-Rasoul family of Thebes, the body of Seti was given into the hands of men who had long forgotten to pay honour to the gods of old Egypt.

And by the impious, yet reverential hands of strangers, the embalmed king was brought from the close-packed burial-chamber of the Her-hor family, in the cliff at Dêr-el-Bahari, and conveyed 450 miles down the Nile to its resting-place in the Bûlâk Museum. Unwrapped as we know it had been at least twice before, by the hands of the priests in the twenty-first dynasty, it had not seen the light for 2913 years—that is, since 1023 B.C. It was finally unwrapped on July 9, 1886; and the mummy-bundle, numbered 3238, gave us back a sight of Seti the king.

This is Professor Maspero's account of the unwrapping, as it appeared in the *Academy* of July 31, 1886 :

"The coffin No. 5232 enclosed the mummy of Seti I., second king of the nineteenth dynasty, and father of Rameses II., according to the *procès verbaux* of the year six and the year sixteen of Her-hor, and of the year ten of Pinotmou I. registered upon the coffin-lid.

"The apparel of bandages and shrouds which enveloped him, was disposed in the same manner as on the mummy of Rameses II.

"Under about half the thickness of linen, were two lines of a hieratic inscription, written in black ink, and informing us that in the year nine, the second month of Puit, the 16th, was the day when the King Menmari (Seti I.) was re-wrapped. Life, health, and strength to the king" (a formula attached to every king, whether living or dead.)

Another inscription, traced on one of the bandages, adds that the linen employed in the enamellings (one does not know what is quite meant—was it the linen used in laying on colour, or linen cartonage?— we expect the latter) had been manufactured by the chief prophet of Ammon, Menkhopirri, in the year five, which gives us the date of the last restoration to which the mummy was subjected.

"The body," continues M. Maspero, "had nearly the same aspect as that of Rameses II.—long, emaciated, of a blackish-yellow colour, the arms crossed upon the chest; the head was covered by a mask of fine linen, blackened with pitch, which had to be lifted up with a chisel.

"Mr. Barsanti, who undertook this delicate operation, brought out of this formless mass the most beautiful mummy's head that has ever been seen in the museum.

"The sculptors of Thebes and Abydos did not flatter Pharaoh when they gave him that delicate, sweet, and smiling profile that travellers admire. The mummy has preserved, after thirty-two centuries, almost the same expression he had when living. What strikes all at first, on comparing it with that of Rameses II., is the astonishing likeness to each other of father and son—nose, mouth, chin; the features are the same, but finer, more intelligent, and more human in the case of the father. Seti. I. is the idealised type of Rameses II. He must have died an old man. The head is shaven; the eyelashes are

white. The state of the body shows him to have
been past his sixtieth year, and this confirms the
opinion of the savants as to his very long reign. The
body is healthy and vigorous, though the knotted
finger-joints bear evident traces of gout. The two
teeth, perceptible under the paste which fills the
mouth, are white and well preserved."

So wrote Maspero the day he first looked Pharaoh
Seti in the face.

When I stood in the hall of mummies at Bûlâk, and
the attendant drew aside the drab veil from the sloping glass case that lay next, and to the right of, the
great Pharaoh of the Bondage, Rameses II., I confess I
did not expect to find such calm beauty and such refinement upon the face of his father, who lay in silence
before me.

The coffin in which the king lay, was thicker in
make, longer and deeper than that of his son, hard
by ; it seemed three inches thick, and had been made
of panels of wood, pegged together, of the same Osirian
type as the other, but clumsier and rougher in build.
I noted that there were five pegs instead of three, for
the fitting on of the coffin-lid.

The coffin's interior had been well daubed with
pitch, and just as was the case in another coffin, the
coffin of the priest Nebseni, some solitary bees had, at
one time or other, built their nests within it.

Looking at the body of the king as he lay amid his

reddish-yellow cerements, one was first struck by the fact that the great coffin somewhat dwarfed the king. His feet did not come to the end of the coffin by nearly a foot and a half; and in the corner was an offering of mummied meat which had perhaps been put there for the food of the soul, either in Amenti, or when it should rise, or perhaps as an offering to the gods when the coffin was last unsealed. It is not unlikely that these coffins were made larger than the mummied forms needed, for the stowing away of all the articles of dress or diet, or tame animal-pets, which it was thought should go along with the dead to the underworld, as was the case with a princess Uast em-Khebit of the Her-hor dynasty of Thebes, who was one of the latest of the royal personages, buried in that wonderful funeral-chamber, wherein the celebrated Dêr-el-Bahari find was made. Her tame gazelle was killed and mummified, and buried along with her, as may be seen any day in the Gîzeh Museum. But to return.

The hands of the king lay crossed, right hand over the left—long, large, powerful hands, swollen somewhat at the joints. The legs and arms still were swathed in the tight-fitting bandages of eternity, but gave one the feeling of being very powerful and robust. He looked as if he had died in his prime.

The wrappings had not been removed from the king's neck, and so there was a life-like proportion given to the head and shoulders, and as one looked the king in the face, one seemed to be gazing on a beautiful statue, hewn from black basalt or ebony. But the face was not the face of one of the sons of Egypt, as we had seen it sculptured and painted and carven in the rooms of the museum that formed the ante-chambers to the Salle des Momies. Turanian, Mongolian, pre-Canaanite, Hyksos, whatever the caste in type was, it was not the ordinary face of the Pharaohs of older or later dynasties that have come down to us. And one saw something in it that made one feel this Set or Setish follower of Baal Sutech, as the name implies, had been born of an alien mother, and had ruled by sheer personal prowess and power over an Egypt, not by tradition of blood his own.

There was quite a remarkable change of colour in the skin, as compared with the lighter yellow face of Rameses II., Seti's son.

There was, speaking broadly, upon Seti's face a sense of wonderful repose—the repose seen upon the face of a good man gone to his rest.

And yet withal there was a kind of look of injured dignity upon it, as if the king had died almost reproaching his death-hour. The face certainly might have smiled often enough in life; but it was a very firm mouth, and it had oftener frowned.

The forehead was shapely—not so retreating as was the forehead of Rameses his son. The head, " dolicho-cephalic," but not to the extent of his son either ;

the ear was delicate, and shone like a bit of polished bog-oak, the nose slightly Napoleonic; the eyebrows, still visible, had been low eyebrows—that is, close above the eyes—heavy and unarched; the eyelashes, by the few remaining hairs, must have been full and long; the lips had projected, without being over-full or fleshy—they did not seem sensual; the cheek-bones were high, and gave a determined look to the face; and again one was impressed by the strength of the jaw, a feature Seti handed on so remarkably to his son.

One other feature was notable: it is a feature which a side view of Rameses' face shows us was a family feature. It is a feature which is observed in nearly all people who are gifted with, or who exercise, strong powers of observation; it is the bar of Michael Angelo. The prominent frontal sinus upon the brow of Seti was most striking. No one who looks upon the un-Egyptian type of face, recovered and brought back to life from its dark sleep of three thousand two hundred and fifty odd years, but must, as he gazes, feel that he is in presence of a gifted maker of history, a great king, ruler, warrior, architect, engineer, in one, who might well have been father of one of the greatest kings the Egyptian people ever knew.

Seti the First, Seti the Truthful, farewell! In whatever larger halls of truth and light your disembodied spirit moves, believe I speak the honest truth, when I say it has been given to few men to die and leave the frail shells of their spirit behind on earth, with such a power to impress the centuries yet unborn, and fill them with the thought that power and refinement, intellect and feeling, must still be the possession of those who would be kings among men.

CHAPTER V

FIRST IMPRESSIONS OF THEBES.

THE great rosy barrier of the Libyan hill, just now apparently right across our path, seemed as the river turned eastward, to come up close, and run parallel with us, and the heights of Kurnet-el-Gûrnah, broken into terraces of yellow-pink limestone, slopes of grey *débris* and shining cliffs of sunny whiteness, became a wall upon our right hand. On our left, the Arabian chain of ghostly lilac hue, rose through the haze in peaks that reminded us of the tent-like shapes of the Cumbrian hills, and seemed to lie beyond a heaving desert of utter barrenness, five miles to the eastward.

The banks of the Nile dwindled, and sloped with gentler slope, and already the husbandmen had utilised the fruitful gift of the gracious river, and the lupin patches and light-green corn and darker clover, had spread a verdurous carpet on either side of the shining water-way. Presently, as we entered upon the " straight " that takes the voyager to Thebes, a voice at my side said, " There is Karnak," and, lifted above the palm groves and acacia trees, dim but forcible, the great square propylon and part of a temple-wall were seen upon the eastern bank. Then, unmistakable among the feathery groves of tall trees, an obelisk was seen.

Karnak was hid behind the palm-grove; at the same time, a brown-looking solid mass, surrounded by what seemed to be a huge mud-wall, was seen, like a blot of shadow upon the sunny treeless plain to the west, and I got my first view of the Temple of Kûrnah, lying in lonely state under the Libyan hill.

It may be well to warn travellers that another " brown-looking mass, surrounded by a mud-wall," does duty on that western side of the plain, for this Temple of Kûrnah. Egyptian sailors are not very particular in details, and often assure the voyager that a substantial looking Shêkh's house across the plain is the ruined " Memnonium of Seti."

But, thought I, surely this is not the Theban plain. " The City of the Hundred Gates " that Homer sang of, was, surely, set round by hills; and here, though it is true that the mountain ranges are visible right and left, there is no circling barrier to keep the world of foes without, the might of wealth within. Rather, the mountains stretch away from the river and leave a plain, right and left, which might in size have given room enough for a city as large as Paris to be built thereon.

But Thebes had its ramparts of old, as Nahum the Prophet knew; "the Rampart of No-Ammon was the sea-like stream," and, certainly, as the river widens out here, one feels almost as if one were sailing on an arm of the sea, rather than an inland river. And yet, withal, there is such tranquillity, such smoothness about its flow, that something of the peace of its dead past enters into one's soul, as one sails on by the palm-groves and the wheat patches, with only the creak of the ceaseless shadûf, to tell one that here still men must labour until the evening, and only in the sweat of their brow eat bread. Let the shadûf-men, as, in their sun-burnt nakedness, they stand and toss their rude buckets from level to level, but cease their work for a week, and the plain that is so fertile, that here, of old, men worshipped the creative principle in nature (made visible under the form of Ammon, or Amen Ra, the Sun-god) would return to the barrenness of the desert, and be naked as the limestone cliffs of the "coffin-mountain," that fence the Theban plain to the west.

But the men who built their "City par excellence," for that is the meaning of Nu, Nua, or, as in the Bible, No, the sacred name of Thebes, chose well. They needed a plain that should be as a garden of Life on the one side of their river, and as a wilderness of Death on the other. So they built their "City of Palaces"—that is the meaning of the modern word

" Luxor," or (Arabic) El-Kusûr—on the eastern bank ;
set up their great temple, their Temple of Ammon, at
Apiu, the City of Thrones, the Karnak of to-day, and
one to the holy Triad of Thebes, at Luxor, and lived
and laboured on the side of the river, where the day-
star rose among the gardens of flowers and groves of
palms ; and over yonder, where all was dry and stark
and treeless, they determined to hide their dead, and
build their memorial temples in honour of the days
that were past, and the deeds done in the flesh ; there,
where the sun went daily to its setting, with hope of a
sure and certain resurrection at the dawn.

Ages have passed over the plain, but life and
activity still remain for the most part, on the eastern
side of the river, and yonder little collection of masts
and boats, beneath the white houses and the palms,
with an obelisk peeping up above the jumble of flat
roofs, and the cornice of the pylon, showing at its
side, tells us that *there* is the City of Palaces. Palaces,
yes, but they are floating ones; they are the State
barges in which the modern tourist finds it convenient
to travel, and there they lie moored, all along the
bank, with their flags of many nations flying, much as
if it were Henley Regatta, or the reach of the Isis at
Oxford, and not the home of the Pharaohs, the haunt
of " Ammon " and " Maut," and " Khons."

The traveller may indeed be forgiven if, as he looks
down the long, still reach of the Nile, up which he

moves towards Thebes, he is disappointed. He knows that, here on this plain a little provincial town grew, under the force of some head-shêkh about 2500 B.C., into a large city; that, before Abraham was, Thebes was great; that though the Shepherd-Kings dispossessed its rulers, and Assur-ban-Nabal sacked it (666 B.C.) and Cambyses swept over it with fire and sword, it survived the shock of ages, long maintained its independence and power of revolt against reigning dynasties, and was not again completely overthrown until the sack of its treasuries and temples, by the vindictive Ptolemy Lathyrus, about 110 B.C.

The traveller has also been told that "no city of the old world can still show so much of her former splendour" as Egyptian Thebes. And so, as he moves up the river through the Theban Plain, and having lost sight of Kûrnah, fails to see any monument on the western plain, except the two black dots that he is told are the colossi, he loses courage. When opposite Apiu, or "Apé," he looks for a Temple on the eastern plain, that enshrined all the highest and best of Egyptian worship to the great Jupiter-Ammon, that was in fact, the centre of religious life of Upper Egypt, from the time of Usertsen I., 2433 B.C., to the time of Alexander, 312 B.C., and only sees what might pass for the dead end-wall of a modern factory, that has been burnt out—his heart fails him. He moves on past the palms, past the "sont" trees, past the tamarisks, and is nearing the home of the most splendid of the splendid Egyptian kings, the glory of the Amenophs and the Ramessids, the pride and honour of the eighteenth and nineteenth dynasties. He is going to land at Luxor, the "city of palaces." He has been told that, at Luxor, is one of the most remarkable temples that modern excavation has made interesting. The temple that the great warrior and architect Amenophis III., built 1500 B.C., that Rameses II. added to, two centuries and a quarter later, and he sees the top of a single obelisk among cheap Arab houses and a squalid mixture of mud and whitewash, and again the traveller's heart dies within him. It was a disappointment to find no shining cliffs, encircling a garden of Paradise, it is a greater, to see no ruins, worthy of the report of its ruined greatness. But the traveller has forgotten that Strabo visited Diospolis, the city of Ammon in 24 B.C. He found it then a place of shattered houses and fallen ruins, and many years have passed since then. Let him take courage, land at the little mud-village, leave the flotilla of house-boats, and, passing through the garden of the new Tewfikieh Hotel—so new that its first crop of beans and cabbages are not, as yet, fully grown—he will find the whole of the mud street torn up, and a great roadway of solid masonry, with isolated blocks twelve feet apart, fringing the solid way. These isolated blocks of limestone are the pediments of the woman-and-ram-

headed sphinxes, which lined the great highway of hewn
 tone, nearly two miles long, which Amenophis III.
made, when he rebuilt the Temple at Luxor 1500 B.C.,
and determined to connect it with the great temple of
Ammon, at Karnak.

We followed this line ourselves, and soon found
that it led up to the huddled Arab quarter of this
" city of palaces," whose nearest approach to a palace
are the pink-hued Italian Consulate and the house of
Mohammed Effendi. Winding through the sinuous
mud street, six or eight feet above the original ram-
sphinx-lined road, we emerged from the huts of the
barbers and the tiny cupboard-shops, where candles
and sugar, and lanterns and linen stuffs, and dried
dates were sold to any one who did not mind a little
Nile-dust being given in with the purchase ; and were
suddenly aware of the fine red granite obelisk, some
eighty-two feet high, that stands where Rameses II.
placed it, in front of the southern pylon of the Temple
of Luxor, somewhere about 1300 years B.C. It struck
me at once as being a splendid piece of workmanship,
the cutting of the inscription quite exquisite in force
and delicacy, but any one who visits Paris can know
something of it, for the obelisk of the Place de la
Concorde, which was its lesser brother, once stood
about twenty paces from this one.

It was a revelation to find what excavations had
done for the magnificent colossi that stand behind

the obelisk, and in front of the Propylon. Familiar
for years past with pictures of this southern gate of
the temple, whereon the heroic single-handed combat
of Rameses II. with the Khita, as sung of by the poet
Pen-ta-Ur, had been engraved, and before which
stood the colossi buried to their chins, one had no idea
of the magnificence of the approach to the large forecourt of Rameses II., till one saw the full height of
the great gate, and its flanking colossal statues of
Pharaoh.   The Talus of the Pylon had been cut
away in two places, to make room, either for other
statues, or for the huge masts that once stood there
for lightning conductors, as some say.   Away down
below, in the great ditch of the excavation, a hundred
Arab lads and lasses, singing their wild work-gang
chant, were to be seen filling the palm-baskets, and
running to tip them into trollies, and thus, each day
to add to the interest of the Temple of Luxor. Poor
little lads and lasses !   The corvée has been done
away with, but not the courbash, and a huge brute of
a Turk lashed out fast and furiously, at the thinly
draped little slaves that passed to and fro, and had it
not been that they laughed and sang as they toiled,
and seemed to take the lash as a matter of course—
something for which they got a piastre and a half
each day—one would have wished all archæological
interest concerning the feet of the colossi and the
lower walls of the propylon, far enough.

Entering into the first court, one noted that it had, with its propylon, been set askew to the main buildings of the earlier temple-body, and this, no doubt, was part of Rameses II.'s design to make it square with the dromos or triumphal way that ran between it and the temple of Karnak; next we observed the seven great statues of the king, that stood between the flanking columns of the southern, eastern and western colonnade, or peristyle, but the chief interest centred in a magnificently wrought statue of Rameses, about twelve feet high, that had escaped the fury of the Persian invader and the savagery of the Copt, and smiled almost, upon the excavators, as they worked, from his position between the glorious columns on the east side of the court.

Quite as beautiful a face of grey granite lies in the deep pit of the excavation to our right hand, as we pass towards the portal that leads to the colonnade of Heru-em-Heb, or Horem-Hib.

I heard that the authorities are about to remove this to the Gîzeh Museum, and have a cast made from it, with which they intend to repair the colossal statue, to which it belongs, and so Rameses will smile serenely, from his royal height as of yore, upon the people passing to and fro to the Temple of Amenoph.

Not one of the least remarkable results of the excavation, is a picture in stone, upon the southern wall of this court, of the propylon, with its colossi and its great bannered masts, as they stood in the days of its builder, so many centuries ago. There is the propylon, there the obelisks, there, four standing colossi, in addition to the two seated ones of to-day, and there the huge masts that took the sunshine in the days when the people passed to worship Ammon Ra, and looked on the Pharaoh Rameses II. as an incarnation of the god of Thebes.

Outside, on the western wall of this court, a battle-scene, or rather one of the old familiar battle-scenes of Rameses' days, has been brought to light. We strolled on through Heru-em-Heb's colonnade, through the court that Seti repaired in the fourteenth century B.C., passed the altar, raised "to the most brave, holy and unconquered Cæsar," and entered the court where Romans once administered justice, and where, while Roman senators stared in togas from the walls of the " cella " in which the Roman emperor's bust stood, the horses champed their bits and stamped in fresco from the side wall.

Thence we wandered into the side-chamber where Queen Maut-em-Shui, the mother of Amenhotep, gives birth to her child, and where two children, perhaps the child and its double, or Ka, are presented on a table of offerings to Ammon Ra, the Theban deity, and so, back to the Sanctuary that " Alexander, the king of men, made for his father Amen-ra, the presiding divinity of Tápé (Thebes). He erected to

him the Sanctuary, a grand mansion, with repairs of
sandstone hewn, good and hard stone, in place of that
made by his majesty Amenhotep, king of men." So
runs the dedication. And so well has the hard stone
of this Sanctuary lasted, that it is as though it were
but put in repair yesterday.

Thence I went to the colonnade, by the banks of
the river, that Amenhotep, king of men, erected somewhere between 1500 and 1510 B.C., for just beyond his
temple lay moored a great raft, whereon were packed
the last consignment of the bodies of the priest-
princes and priestesses of the twentieth dynasty, that
had just been conveyed from their long rest in a
tomb-chamber near the Dêr-el-Bahari, and I was
anxious to learn from the director of the Gîzeh
Museum, some particulars of this latest important find.

Mons. Grébaut received me courteously. " But,"
said he, " you are just a week too late. A fortnight
ago yesterday, we took from the tomb the first of the
mummies which came up to the light, a little child—
and a week ago yesterday, the last was conveyed across
the Theban plain in safety, to the raft we had prepared,
whereon to despatch the bodies down Nile to Cairo,
the last of one hundred and sixty-three coffin-cases, of
which, not more than twelve had been tampered with
at all." My courteous informant showed me that it was
a most important find. The twentieth dynasty was an
age of transition, of which we know little. It is not,

of course, so remarkable a discovery in the actual personages; but it is likely enough, from a cursory examination, that some of the mummies are of royal birth. Such names as Pinothem, Masahirta, Hontet-chui and Nessichonsu, look as if some members of the reigning families may be expected to be amongst those brought to light.

It is true that there have been found sixteen canopic jars, one hundred ushabti boxes, containing close on one thousand blue porcelain figures, pots of honey, dôm-palm fruit, muslin, mummied meats, and two very curious white-painted figures, with outstretched hands, of Nephthys and Isis. Nor should one omit mention of two palm-fans or flabella, and a pair of sandals upon which the mud of ages ago may still be seen sticking; but these are not the objects that give us hope that this discovery will be, historically, of great worth.

The interest of the find, centres in the papyri, seventy-seven osiris boxes, of which, seventy-five contain rolls of papyrus, some of great length; these will, we trust, when unrolled, tell us a good deal of the condition of the religion, perhaps of the condition of the people. One priest is spoken of as "general of the auxiliary forces of Thebes;" we may, perhaps, find civil and military matters dealt with, and, at least, may hope to find hiati in our knowledge of the ritual of Thebes, in the times of the twentieth dynasty, filled up, perhaps discover further chapters in the Book of the Dead.

The next day I visited the pit whence the mummies were taken, and fell in with the Arab jackal-hunter, Abd er-Rasoul, to whom, if one may trust his word, Egyptologists are indebted for this new addition to the roll of history. He grinned, and told me he had known of this great vault of mummies for fifteen years past, and when I asked him how he had discovered it, he said, pointing to the iron probing-rod he held in his hand, " With this."

The pit's mouth lay about 200 yards to the north-west of the lower terrace of the Dêr-el-Bahari.

The pit was about 10 feet square, and went down, without masonry on either side of it, far into the ground for a depth of 45 feet ; thence a gallery, about 12 feet wide by 6 feet, had been hewn, that ran north and south, and had a side gallery midway of 65 feet. The total length of the main gallery was roughly 424 feet, and this was crowded with the mummy-cases of those one hundred and sixty-three priests and priestesses of the twentieth dynasty. The sight of the removal of these mummies in their coffins across the Theban plain was, so all who witnessed it tell me, most remarkable. Twice in each day, a funeral procession of six or ten bodies borne upon biers, by ten or twelve men each, moved down through the sands of Assasîf, to the green cornfields of the

Ramesseum, and so, across the plain, to the creeks of
the Nile and the sandy flat that lies opposite Luxor.

And now part of the august assembly of priests and
priestesses, who knew the Temples in their grandeur,
and worshipped Amen Ra 1200 to 1000 years B.C.,
have passed down the river to the Gîzeh Museum,
and part are on a raft, almost within shadow of the
Colonnade that Heru-em-Heb built 3350 years ago, at
Luxor, and wait for the steamer that shall tear them
away for ever, from the scenes of their life and love
and labour, and the home, as they had hoped, of their
eternal sleep. Let us hope the world will be the
wiser and their loss of rest, our gain. It is but right
to say that, whatever claim Abd er-Rasoul may advance as to his knowledge of the whereabouts of the
actual pit, in which these wonderful mummies of the
priests and priestesses of the nineteenth and twentieth
dynasty were hid, he knew nothing of the actual contents of the gallery, forty-five feet underground, and
it was the scientific narrowing of the area of search,
carried on by Mons. Grébaut, who has entered so
ably upon the previous work of Messrs. Maspero and
Mariette, that has really been the cause of the great
find. Mons. Grébaut knew that a little area, in a line
of important tombs, had been unworked, and he set to
work thereon, with the result that these 163 bodies
have been recovered. The mummy cases, or coffins,
themselves are full of interest even in their very

ornaments, for they introduce symbols and figures as yet unknown. I saw, for example, upon six of them a winged ox, which was novel in such ornament. The coffins themselves look as if they were painted and varnished only yesterday. The priests are darker skinned, in face than the priestesses, that is, as represented on the coffin lids—the ladies for the most part have head-dresses of blue-green, or green-blue, and wear earrings. The coffins of the twentieth dynasty are, for the most part, painted with figures on a white ground, the coffin cases of the twenty-first dynasty are painted with green and blue and black and red, upon a yellow ground.

They vary in size. Some are evidently the mummy-cases of little children; some are more than a ton in weight, and required twelve men to lift them.

As for the papyri, which really constitute the main interest of the discovery, they are enclosed in osiris boxes, some of which stood as much as three feet high, and this means that they are papyri of great size. There may, of course, be many other papyri wrapped up with the mummies themselves, it is enough to know that those already found in the hollow osiride-figure boxes have, for the most part, never been unsealed, since the day they were deposited in the mummy-pit, and the world of Egyptologists will be anxious to know their contents, which Mons. Grébaut will as soon as possible examine, and make known. Mons. Daressy was the engineer in charge of the lifting of the coffins to the pit's mouth, and such care was used, and such expedition, that in a single week, the whole number of mummy-cases had been conveyed without damage to the raft at Luxor.

Many a time, after that first day at Luxor, did I wander by that solid memorial of the last king of the eighteenth dynasty—the colonnade of Heru-em-Heb ; and, passing across the river, gaze back at it, in its hour of beauty, that witching hour of the Theban sunset. Often did I pass along the newly-excavated, western wall of the temple, and look upon the pictures of horsemen and chariots on warlike expeditions, in a mountainous country. Sometimes, leaving the so-called Christian church inside the walls, I passed to the little baptistry of the early Copts, the excavators had laid bare, and puzzled over the plant and tree life which the men of an earlier day had carved upon the walls hard by ; not seldom did one return to the forecourt of Rameses, and notice how the king who designed it had been obliged, up to the central pillar, to enclose a portion of the sphinx-avenue of Amenophis, and had, by reason of this fact, been compelled to set his pylons askew, so as to secure a central approach for the dromos which united his temple-building with Karnak. Nor could one help wondering at the skill of the obelisk-hewers of

M

Rameses' day, who knew that under the bright sun, if the sides of the obelisk had been absolute planes, they would, by reason of the sharpness of the corners, have appeared slightly concave, and who, to avoid this optical delusion and to satisfy the eye, had given a slight entasis or convexity to the surfaces, which was gradually diminished towards the point. What a pity it seemed as one stood facing the now unburied propylon and forecourt, that modern Luxor should prevent for years to come—perhaps for ever—anything like a sufficient clearance of ground, to enable us to judge of the grandeur of the temple approach, as known to the men of the eighteenth and nineteenth dynasties. Often with one's mind full of the poem of Pen-ta-ur, and its illustrations on the walls, one would go and look at the picture in the many-statued court of the dedication of the temple to Amen-Ra, look upon the great religious procession, the sons of the king—the Pharaoh of the Exodus among them, thirteenth in the upper register—and marvel at the fatness of the prize-fed, heavy-belled, and high-plumed oxen that went on that occasion to the sacrifice; how their tongues lolled out, how hot and fat they seemed !

Sometimes, when the light was good, one returned to that strange bridal-chamber at the north-east end of the Macedonian sanctuary, and marvelled at the quaint wall-pictures of the wooing of a mortal queen

by the great god. The conception, the birth of the
child, the dedication of its "double" to the heavenly
father, the caresses and tender affection bestowed
upon it by its earthly parent, set forth in mystic wise,
were pictures as full of interest as they were difficult
with certainty to interpret; and it was with a kind of
relief that one turned back towards the central hall,
by way of the black granite foundation-stones, that
tell us how long before Amenoph's time here Sebek-
em-Saf built his temple to the Theban god, and saw
upon the walls slaves staggering under their gigantic
oil jars, or bearing, as a present to the god, one of
the caged lions which Amen-hetep III. had brought
from the hunting-field; for Amenoph, the knightly, the
generous and the brave, was the Nimrod of Egypt,
and could boast, as his "Scarabæi" tells us, that in
the first ten of his thirty-five years reign, he had slain
one hundred and two lions with his own hand.

I have sometimes wondered whether those five hundred and seventy-two statues of the lioness-headed
wife of Ptah, Sekhet-Pasht, whose few remaining
figures lean so sorrowfully round the sacred lake of
what was once the temple to Mut, which Amen-hetep
built to the right of his ram-sphinx avenue at Karnak,
may not have had their origin in some wish to memo-
rialise the lion-hunter's prowess. It certainly was his
love of the lion-hunt which won for him the love of
Taia. What a fine couple they must have been!

Any one who remembers the refinement of the face of Amenoph III., as seen to-day in stone in the British Museum ; any one who has once gazed upon the face of his Mesopotamian consort, which looks down upon us in its white limestone loveliness in the hall at Gîzeh, will understand this.

One can see them borne by barge, or carried on litters to the terrace by the Nile bank, with their attendant officers and fan-bearers, and a goodly company, in the days of auld lang syne, to watch the masons at their work of rearing the last of the thirty-two columns that should perpetuate their piety and their splendour. By their side stands the architect, Amen-hotep, son of Hapoo, just fresh come from the sandstone quarries of Silsileh, where he is hewing the twin Colossi for his royal master, and full of enthusiasm about the eight gigantic rafts which he has planned for their transport. The dream fades, dispelled by the clouds of dust that rise from the trenches of excavation round this ancient hall ; but I expect even to-day, in spirit, that royal pair might be with us in our unfeigned satisfaction to witness the carefulness with which M. Grébaut, director of Egyptian antiquities, is doing all he can to recover for us, the history of the temple of Amen-Ra at Luxor, and with careful repair, is giving back to the pillars of Amenoph something of their original strength and beauty. These pillars of the Central Hall at Luxor

have stood nigh upon 3400 years, and if only the
constantly rising level of the Nile will admit of it, they
may stand as long again.

Every day that the traveller stays at Luxor, Luxor
and its surroundings of wonder and beauty grow upon
him ; but nothing will quite efface his first impression
of Thebes as he sails up the river to the mooring, and
that impression is almost certain to be one of disappointment.

CHAPTER VI.

THE silence of Egypt to-day is very impressive : the songlessness of the land lays a heavy weight upon one. The cry of the hoopoe, the chirrup of the quail, the burr of the sákiyeh, the bark of a village dog, and the melancholy pastoral pipe of a shepherd in mid-plain—these come to one as a surprise and pleasure. But the silence of the dead soon swallows up all these living sounds, and one would give, at times, a good deal to hear even a German band or a hurdy-gurdy. This was not so in the olden time. Then, when the boat-loads passed along the Nile there was song. The pipers played lustily, as the pilgrims floated on to their yearly festival at Bubastis.

Every temple, with the exception of the temple to Osiris at Abydos, had its trained band of music makers and singers. No feasts, funeral or otherwise, were complete without the sound of harp and pipe, lyre, guitar, tambourine, and flute.

Plato tells us that music was considered, by the

Egyptians, as a most important factor in the education of children. Strabo informs us that the scholars were taught not only their letters, but songs appointed by law, and a certain kind of music established by government. And though it would appear that the higher classes were not in the habit of performing in public, but left that to a great professional class of musicians, there are evidences on the walls of the tombs that even the priestly caste gave musical " at homes."

Visitors to Tell el-Amarna may remember the picture of the blind Egyptian harper and his chorus of blind singers (Sir G. Wilkinson, " Ancient Egyptians," vol. ii. p. 95). They will have noted in the so-called Tomb of the Harper, the tomb of Rameses III. at Thebes, the grace and size of the harp that made sweet music, 1200 B.C. They will remember that Thothmes III. (1600 B.C.), the king who began the building of that great hall of columns at Karnak, appointed feasts of victory to be celebrated on the festivals of Amen Ra. Amongst the treasures and gifts to the god's shrine of which we have record, special mention is made of a beautiful harp of silver and gold and precious stones " to sing the praises of Amen upon his splendid festival days." But the days of music, " that fair handmaiden of God and near allied unto divinity," have an ancestry in Egypt that reaches back beyond the pyramid days ; and the traveller who, after gazing at the sistrum and pipe and harp and viol that may be seen in the

Egyptian collection of the British Museum, goes to Egypt and is at the trouble of visiting the Mêdûm will find that in the time of Seneferu the favourite guitar of old Egypt has become a symbol for words, has already passed into speech as the word "Nefer," and is carved next to the sickle, upon the huge lintel of the doorway of the Lady Atot's tomb. The hymnody of ancient Egypt was a national possession. The psalm-singing of the Hebrews who came up out of Egypt, is little to be wondered at by those who note how on the monuments the voice and instruments seem to go together. The tunes are lost, but some of the familiar hymns of that old people of the Nile, preserved to us in papyri, and now done into verse, may be of interest to the reader.

It has seemed a pity that the most authentic prose translations of the hymns, dirges, poems, and wise sayings of Ancient Egypt should, by reason of their unmusical form, remain comparatively unknown to the general reader.

I have attempted, as literally as I can, to render a few of them in metre, in the hope that they may thereby become more popular with the traveller to Egypt.

The hymns have been placed chronologically, but the " Heroic Poem of Pen-ta-ur," as being distinct in character, has been printed at the end of Chapter VI. "The Precepts of Ptah-hotep" stand by themselves in a separate chapter.

THE FESTAL DIRGE OF KING ANTEF.

ELEVENTH DYNASTY, 2533–2466 B.C.

THIS solemn festal dirge, of which a free rendering is here given, was found among the Harris papyri. By the first lines of the hymn, its authorship is ascribed to King Antef, or Antuf, one of the Pharaohs of the eleventh dynasty, whose humble brick tombs have been discovered at Drah Abu'l Nekkah, at Thebes, and specimens of whose coffins may be seen in the Louvre, and at the British Museum. The stele of King Antef will be familiar to visitors to the Gîzeh Museum. It is, at any rate, allowable for us, as we gaze upon that worthy, well-wigged prince sitting in his chair, beneath which his favourite hound is on guard, and behind which stand the great man's slipper-bearer and fly-flapper, to believe that we are in presence of the author of this venerable poem. A little imagination might make us think that he who on that stele is seen just to be reaching out his hand to take a cup of wine, whilst the banquet of "all good things in abundance," is within arm's reach, was himself in the habit of acting up to the advice he gives his friends, and had felt, sadly enough, that it was best to make the most of the good things the gods had sent.

Be that as it may, no one who reads this pathetic dirge, which, for so many hundred years in Egypt, gave its poor comfort or hopeless encouragement to those who came together to the funeral feasts, or listened to its after-dinner melody, will forget that Herodotus probably heard it sung on one of the occasions he describes in his Euterpe, chap. 28, as follows : " At the entertainments of the rich, just as the company is about to rise from the repast, a small coffin is carried round, containing a perfect representation of a dead body. It is in size sometimes of one, but never more than two cubits, and as it is shown to the guests, one after one, the bearer exclaims : " Cast your eyes on this figure. After death you yourself will resemble it. Drink, then, and be happy."

We have, probably, here a well-known Egyptian festal dirge written, say, 1600 years before great Homer lived and sung, for we cannot assign a later date than 2466 B.C. to the close of that shadowy eleventh dynasty of the Antefs, who ruled at Thebes.

The papyrus from which Mr. C. W. Goodwin translated the dirge is of later date—viz., of the time of Thothmes III., of the eighteenth dynasty, 1600 B.C. ; but this only goes to prove how favourite a hymn for tomb-festivals this was among the Egyptians for centuries. That there were many copies of it may be inferred from the fact that one other is still in existence, and is deposited in the Leyden Museum. For Mr. Goodwin's translation of the dirge *cf.* " Records of the Past," vol. iv. p. 117, or *Trans. Soc. Bib. Archæol.* vol. iii. pt. 1.

FESTAL DIRGE OF KING ANTEF.

2533–2466 B.C.

The Festal Dirge of Antef, king, deceased,
Writ clear before the player on the harp.

HAIL the good man and the great,
    Hail the worthy passed away;
Men of poor or proud estate
    Find one end—the clay.

What is fortune? say the wise.*
    Vanished are the hearths and homes,
What he does or thinks, who dies,
    None to tell us comes.

Have thy heart's desire, be glad,
    Use the ointment while you live;
Be in gold and linen clad,
    Take what gods may give.

---

* Literally, I have heard the words of Imhotep and Hartatef.
It is said in their sayings, "After all, what is prosperity?"
Imhotep, the son of the primeval deity Ptah, was the mythical
author of arts and sciences. Hartatef was the son of Menkaura,
the builder of the third pyramid, to whom the discovery of part
of the "Ritual," chap. lxiv., was attributed. These references
are indications of the great antiquity of this dirge.

For the day shall come to each
   When earth's voices sound no more ;
Dead men hear no mourners' speech,
   Tears cannot restore.

Eat and drink in peace to-day,
   When you go, your goods remain ;
He who fares the last, long way,
   Comes not back again.

THE SONG OF THE HARPER.

EIGHTEENTH DYNASTY, 1700–1400 B.C.

THE song was evidently rhythmic, and was written in verses of equal length :

> " Ured urui pu mā
> Pa shau nefer kheper
> Khetu her sebt ter rek Rā
> Jamāu her at r ast-sen."

The literal translation into English we subjoin, keeps both the verse and the metre as near as may be ; and, as will be noticed, evidently goes to a harp accompaniment.

The original was found in the tomb of Nefer Hotep at Abd el-Kûrnah, near Thebes, and is a good specimen of Egyptian poetry of the eighteenth dynasty, 1700 to 1400 B.C.

It is a funeral song supposed to be sung by a harper at the anniversary or feast in remembrance of the death of the patriarch Neferhotep, who is represented sitting with his sister and wife, Rennu-m-ast-neh, his son Ptahmes and his daughter Ta-khat standing by their side, while the harper before them is chanting. The poet addresses his words to the dead, as well as the living, assuming in his fiction that the former is still alive. The dirge may well be compared with the Festal Dirge of King Antef. This rendering into verse is from the translation of Ludwig Stern in " Records of the Past," vol. vi. p. 127.

THE SONG OF THE HARPER

1700–1400 B.C.

This is the song the harper used to sing
In the tomb chapel of the Osirian,
The blessed Neferhotep, Amen's Priest.

NEFERHOTEP, great and blest,
　　Of a truth is sleeping;
We as surety for his rest
　　All good charges keeping.
Since the day when Ra and Tum
　　Ran his first of races,
Fathers pass, and after come
　　Children in their places.
Certain as great Ra* appears,
　　Sires are sons begetting,
Man begets and woman bears
　　Sure as Tum† is setting.
Breezes from the morning blown
　　Every man inhaleth,
To his place then going down,
　　Woman-born, he faileth.

---

* Ra : The sun-god generally.
† Tum : The sun at its setting.

II.

May this day in joy return,
    Speed it, holy father ;
Scent these oils we pour and burn,
    Take the flowers we gather.
In thy heart, as in thy shrine,
    See thy sister dwelling;
Round her arms and bosom twine
    Lotus flowers, excelling.
Lo ! she sits beside thee close ;
    Let the harp delight thee ;
Let our singing banish woes,
    Leave the cares that spite thee.
Joy thee till the pilgrim band
    One day shall have started,
Entering to thy silent land,
    Welcome, and long-parted.

III.

That this day with joy may speed,
    Patriarch, grant assistance ;
Whole of heart and pure of deed
    Past from earth's existence.
His life shared the common lot,
    Here is no sure dwelling ;
He who just now was, is not,
    And his place past telling.

N

So it has been since the sun
  Rose, so must be, O man !
Eyes just open, then as one
  Never born of woman.
In the shades, upon the brink
  Of the sacred river,
'Mid the ghosts thy soul doth drink
  Draughts of life for ever.

IV.

If when harvest fails, the poor
  Cry to thee for feeding,
Give, so honoured evermore
  Shall thy name be speeding.
Give, so to thy funeral feast
  Crowds will come, adoring ;
In his panther skin, the priest *
  Wine to thee outpouring.
Cakes of bread and staves of song
  Will be thine, elected
Stand before god Ra, the throng
  Of thy friends, protected.
Harvests duly shall return,
  Nor by Shu† forsaken ;
While in hell the lost ones burn,
  Glorious shalt thou waken.

---

* Priests of " Chem, the Vivifier," wore the panther skin.
† Shu : **Dryness** sunlight, the fruitful principle in air.

V.

Neferhotep, pure of hand,
  Speed the day we pray thee;
Not the buildings thou hast planned
  Could avail to stay thee.
All his wealth this little earth
  For his rest containeth,
This poor ash is all his worth—
  Look ye! what remaineth.
When the moments came that he
  Sought the realms of heaven,
Not one jot might added be,
  Not one moment given.
They whose barns are crammed with corn,
  One day make a finish;
Death will laugh their wealth to scorn,
  Death their pride will 'minish.

VI.

Friends, ye all one day go hence:
  Be your hearts discerning;
Mind ye of the bourne from whence
  There is no returning.
Honest lives will then have proved
  Gain, but loathe transgressing;
Be ye just, for justice, loved,
  Brings a good man blessing.

Be we coward, be we brave,
    Rich in friends, forsaken ;
None of us escape the grave—
    All alike are taken.
Give, of thine abundance give !
    And to truth attending,
Blest by Isis shalt thou live
    Happy, to thine ending.

HYMN OR ODE TO PHARAOH.

NINETEENTH DYNASTY, 1400–1200 B.C..

THIS hymn is from the Anastasi papyri, and, though undated, is believed to belong to the nineteenth dynasty. It is interesting for two reasons.

It shows how entirely the king of that day had been identified with the sun, as a divinity, or rather as a living image or incarnation of the sun-god, and suggests that the Pharaoh Meneptah, Baenra-Meriamun, the immediate successor of Rameses II., was living at a time when it was very necessary to have a close watch kept upon the doings of his people, or part of his people, and apparently, at a time when some great conspiracy had just been discovered, and brought to the notice of him who "had millions of ears," and whose eye saw "everything that was done in secret."

If the Pharaoh, addressed in this hymn, was indeed the Pharaoh of the Bondage, we may guess what that conspiracy was, and read the hymn with added interest, in the light that is let in upon the god-king's character, by the Hebrew Scriptures.

For the prose form of which this is a metrical rendering *cf.* Mr. C. W. Goodwin's translation, "Records of the Past," vol. vi. p. 101.

HYMN OR ODE TO PHARAOH MENEPTAH.

1300 B.C.

Long live the king !
As ambassadors we bring
Message to the royal hall
Where he reigns, truth's loving lord ;
Message to the sun's house, heaven :
Let thine ear to us be given,
Thou great orb that, rising, brightens
And enlightens
Earth with all
His gifts of good outpoured.
Thou the image art of him
Who doth rise with morning's glow.
Into caverns dark and dim
Gleams the glory of thy face.
Thou dost speak, and worlds obey.
Even in thy sleeping-place,
In thy palace, thou canst know
What all people say.
Million-eared, thine eye is bright,
Brighter than the morning star,
Strong to gaze upon the sun.
Privy whisperings that are

Muttered in the caves beneath,
Straight into thine ear ascend.
Yea, all things in secret done
Come into thy sight,
Oh Baenra Meriamun,
Thou of mercy lord and friend
Thou dost give us breath.

THE DIRGE OF MENEPTAH.

NINETEENTH DYNASTY, 1400–1200 B.C.

IT is uncertain to which monarch of the nineteenth dynasty this dirge is addressed. The Papyrus Anastasi No. 4, British Museum, may belong to the reign either of Rameses II., the Pharaoh of the Bondage, 1333 B.C., or Seti II. Meneptah III., 1266 B.C. Of the latter Pharaoh, though he appears to have reigned thirty-three years, there are, according to Brugsch, no records after the first two years of his reign ; hence it is impossible, from the allusion to his triumph over the " Syrians " and " negroes " in the poem, to determine to which of the Pharaohs the dirge belongs. Nor is there anything upon the walls of his little temple, lately unearthed, to the north-west of the great front court at Karnak, so far as I could discover, to throw light upon the poem ; but the first line of the dirge may allude to Seti's interest in Karnak, and the building of that little three-chambered temple. It is probable that Seti II. was a lover of literature, for that beautiful tale of the " Two Brothers," with its parallel to a passage in the history of Joseph (*cf.* " Records of the Past," vol. ii. p. 137), was written specially for him when he was a crown prince. His sepulchre in Bibân el-Mulûk, at Thebes, is certainly much more magnificent than is the uninteresting tomb of Rameses II. One must not press this, but the poem contains the suggestion that the king was literary, and had a magnificent tomb. The poetical rendering follows the text of the translation by S. Birch, LL.D, "Records of the Past," vol. iv. p. 51.

THE DIRGE OF MENEPTAH.

1333–1266 B.C.

AMEN gladdened thine heart,
Gave thee a good old age,
Pleasure followed thee near,
Thy words were the words of a sage;
Sound was thine arm, and clear
Thine eye, its arrows could dart;
Now thou art gone to the breaks
In the West, where the sun-boat takes
The dead, for Amenti who steer.
Thou hast guided thy golden car,
With the whip in thine hand thou hast gone,
Yoked were thy horses, and followed
Thy triumph, the Syrian foe
And the negroes taken in war,
Proof of the deeds thou hast done.
So to thy boat didst thou go,
Thy boat of acacia-wood hollowed;
So to the tower of thy home,
Built by thine hand, didst thou come.
Then was their sacrifice—bread,
Wine, and meat for thy mouth;

The ox was felled, and the jar
Broached, and we sang thee a song.
The anointer anointed thine head
With balsam fresh from the South ;
All the pool-flowers that blow
The chief of thy gardeners brought ;
All the winged fowls we know
The chief of thy bailiffs had caught—
Offerings fair for thy wish,
And thy fishermen brought to thee fish.
Came on thy tomb-chapel wall
Thy galley from Syria along,
Laden with spoils that were good ;
Horses were there in thy stall,
And there thy slave-maidens stood,
Slave-maidens helpful and strong ;
And ever beneath thy sword
Were thine enemies seen to fall ;
None were opposed to thy word.
But lo ! to the judgment-hall
Of Osiris now thou art gone,
Victor and justified one.

HYMN TO AMEN RA.

NINETEENTH DYNASTY, 1400–1200 B.C.

THIS celebrated hymn, of which a rendering is given, is taken from papyrus No. 17 in the Gîzeh Museum, a facsimile of which has been published by M. Mariette.

It is contained in a papyrus of small size, in eleven pages of moderate length, and has the advantage of being written in a legible hand ; it is almost perfect, and is free from any great difficulties for the translator. The beginning of each verse is indicated in the original, by small rubricated letters.

From the handwriting, it is judged to belong to the nineteenth dynasty, the dynasty that gave us Seti I. and his son, the Pharaoh of the Bondage, Rameses II., but it purports to be a copy of a much older composition. Doubtless it is a hymn which was in common use at both centres of sun-worship—Karnak, or Aptu, and An, or Heliopolis ; for all we know, it may have been used from the time of Usertsen, of the twelfth dynasty, onwards—*i.e.*, from 2400 B.C. to the end of the Egyptian dynasties.

It has all the appearance of being a liturgical

hymn, that had many additions made to it, and if we complain of the weariness of its repetitions, we have but to think of the liturgies of the Western Church, to see how naturally these additions would be made. The dominant note of the absolute oneness, the unity of the godhead of Amen Ra under all his forms, is very remarkable. There is throughout, some awkwardness of expression which the literal translator cannot escape from, by reason of the way in which, whilst now and again the god is addressed in the first person, there is always a swift transition to the third person—a hint, perhaps, of that awe in which the deity was held, and which allowed the worshipper to speak of, rather than to, the divine one.

Readers should compare Mr. C. W. Goodwin's translation of this famous hymn, as given in "Records of the Past," vol. ii. p. 129, with the admirable version, by Mr. Wallis Budge, of M. Grébaut's later translation, as given in "Notes for Travellers in Egypt," p. 80.

HYMN TO AMEN RA.*

1400–1200 B.C

I.

PRAISE to Amen Ra we give,
First of gods, in An the bull,
Lord beloved and beautiful,
By whose warmth fair cattle live;
Hail the king of double throne,
Chief in Karnak; of his fields

---

* Amen Ra was said to be the son of Ptah, or Vulcan, whose chief place of honour and worship was Memphis.

Originally a local deity, Amen Ra became in later times, from the twelfth dynasty onward, a god of great importance, and his worship culminated, probably about the nineteenth dynasty.

He was adored at An, or Heliopolis, the university city of Moses' time; but the chief seat of his worship was Thebes, or Karnak, called in this hymn Apts, or Aptu.

Here at "Apts," with Mut and Chonsu as other persons of the Theban triad, Amen Ra was the presiding deity. All that splendour of building could do, was done from the time of Amen-nemhat I., 2466 B.C., to the time of the Ptolemies, to give him honour.

He is represented on the monuments as wearing the tall feathers of law or justice in his crown, and as holding the scourge of rule, the crook of dominion, the hooked sceptre of power, and the tower of stability.

Mighty head ;
Bull, by whom himself was bred,
Stretching out his feet afar
Proudly to the southern zone,
Proudly o'er the Asian plains,*
Lord and Prince of Araby,
Lord of all the breadth of sky,
Earth's first son ;
Lord of things that are,
Great creator who sustains
All that earth or heaven yields.

II.

One in time and works among
The high gods' throng,
Beautiful,
The mighty bull,
'Mid the gods pre-eminent,
Lord of law, and president,
Father of the gods and men,
Maker of the beasts that be,
Lord of all existences,
Giver of the fruitful trees,
Filling house and cattle-pen
With the staff of daily food.
Son of Vulcan, fair and good,
Lo ! the gods adore and love,

---

* Māt'au, a country in Asia.

By the gods is honour paid
To the god who all things made—
Things below and things above.
Lo, he passes through the sky,
Sailing in tranquillity,
Blessing both the lands with light,
King of north and king of south,
Giving law with truthful mouth,
Prince of this world, great in might
Lord of terror and affright—
He who takes
The earth, and makes
It like to his divinity.

III.

He hath forms, yea, very many,
More than any
Other god.
In his beauties gods rejoice,
To his praise they lift their voice
And adore his name,
When he comes from his abode,
Rising crowned with flame,
Glorious the two lands above.
He whose fragrances they love,
Incense-born and dewy-sweet,
When he comes from Araby,
When his feet
Over plains of Asia fly,

And his smile
Beams along the land divine,*
Where the Red Sea waters shine,
Southward of the land of Nile.

IV.

At his feet the gods attend,
In acknowledgment they bend
To his awful majesty.
Lord of fear and victory,
Mighty one of will,
Master of the crowns, and king,
Making green the offering,
Giver of the holy food,
Pure and good.
We adore with salutation
Thee who called into creation
Even the gods; thy skill,
In love,
Hath outstretched the heavens above,†
And hath set the earth's foundation !

V.

Tireless watcher, Amsu‡ Amen,
Lord of all eternity,

---

* Neter-ta—that is, *divine land*—the name given on the monuments to indicate the lands which lie to the south of Egypt
between the Nile and the Red Sea.   † *Cf.* Psalm cx. 3.
  ‡ Amsu was one of the forms of Amen Ra.

Maker of the lasting morns,
Prayer and praises rise to thee !
Thou the head of Karnak, Ra ! men
Bow before thee
And adore thee,
Beautiful with double horns.
Lord of the Uræus crown,
Plumed, exalted high to wear
Snow-white helm, tiara fair,
With the grace
Of the serpent, and the disk
Of the double basilisk,
As adornment to his face.
In his own
Temple are his emblems known,
Helmet-cap and double crown
Lo, benign of face, he deigns
Take the Atef crown* in hands,
Crowned with Sechti crown † he stands,
And as lord of life he reigns
With the lotus-handled rod
And the scourge, ‡ a sceptred god.

---

* The *Atef crown* is the curious double-plumed crown above
ram's horns which Khnemu is generally seen to wear.

† The *Sechti crown* is made up by a conjunction of the red and
the white crowns of Upper and Lower Egypt. Horus is generally
represented as wearing it.

‡ This is the scourge growing out of a lotus, called the

VI.

Gracious Ruler, rising bright,
Crowned with crown of silver white,
Lord of rays,
Great creator of the light,
Unto him the gods give praise,
And he stretches from above
Hands of love to them that love ;
But the rebels fall, his eyes
Fiercely flame upon the foe.
See, his arrows pierce the skies
With their ruddy glow,
And the Nāka * serpent flies,
And disgorging dies
In the dark below.

VII.

Hail to thee, Lord God of law,
Thee whose shrine none ever saw ;

Amsu sceptre, which is held by Amen Ra, who is addressed as
Amsu Amen.

* Nāk, another name for Āpepi, the demon-serpent of cloud
and mist and night, who is generally represented with knives or
daggers stuck into his back. He was supposed to swallow up
the sun daily, and during the hours of darkness the battle between the sun-god Ra and the terrible serpent was supposed to
be going on, but the sun was always victorious; Āpepi or Nāk
was vanquished; night fled away, and morning appeared in the
east.

Lord of gods, God-Chepera,*
Sailing in thy boat along,
By whose word the great gods are.
Thee we hail in song
Atmu,† maker of mankind.
Forms to all the men that be,
Colour and variety,
By his fiat are assigned.
Unto him the poor men cry,‡
And he helps them in distress ;
Kind of heart is he to all
Who upon him call,
God Almighty to deliver
Him that is afraid and meek,
From the great ones who oppress,
Judging ever
'Twixt the strong and weak.

VIII.

Of intelligence the Lord,
Wisdom ever is the word
That his mouth doth give.
At his will the Nile-god moves,
And that lord the palm-tree loves,

---

* Creator.

† Atmu, the "closer," was the form under which the setting sun was worshipped.

‡ *Cf.* Psalm xxxiv. 17 ; xxxv. 10.

Comes to make us mortals live.
He all work on earth advances,
Working with us in the sky,
Everything that loves the light
Leaps to meet him,
And rejoicing in his glances,
Beauteous, bright,
All gods greet him,
Glad at heart when he is by.

IX.

Ra, in Karnak mighty lord,
When he rises in his shrine;
Āni,* lord of those who shout
When the new moon's horns do shine;
When the six days have increased
His silver rim,
Thou dost for him
Make the feast;
When the moon is fading out,
Still thou art adored.
Prince! life, health, and strength to thee!
Lord of gods, whose rising flame
Smiles along the level land!
President of those who sleep †
With our fathers in the sand;

---

* Āni is one of the forms of the sun-god **Ra**.
† Auker, a common name for a necropolis.

Lo ! his name from us is deep-
Hidden in his secret name
Amen *—none may understand.

x.

Hail thou joyous Sun, to thee
In thy pure tranquillity ;
Lord of all hearts' exaltation,
Lord of crown, whose decoration
Are the plumes, and fair to see
With tiara, and the tall
Milk-white helm ; the gods above
Look upon thy face with love,
With the double crown of power,
Crown of Upper, crown of Lower
Egypt, on thy brow,
Passing thro' the double lands.
Sending forth when thou dost rise
Love-looks from thy lovely eyes.
Lo ! the dead men in the sands
Are in raptures of delight
When thou risest, shining bright ;
When thou burnest at the noon,
Cattle faint and swoon.
Loved thou art when in the south
Thou thy might art pouring forth,
When thou shinest in the north
Ah ! how pleasant is thy mouth.

---

* Amen, hidden.

Lo ! the beauties of thy face
Steal the hearts of all away ;
Yea, for love of thee our arms
Fail, we tremble at thy charms,
And the glory of thy grace
Melts us day by day.

XI.

Form The All-Creator, One !
Maker of existences !
Men came forth from his two eyes,
From his mouth the gods began.
For the ox, he is the giver
Of green herb—of corn, for man ;
By him fishes fill the river,
Wingèd fowl fill the sky ;
To the egg its being's breath
He ordaineth ;
And sustaineth
Things that creep on earth beneath,
Things that upward fly ;
Even for the rats that run
To their hiding-holes, the sun
Bringeth food, and to the nest
Where the sweet birds rest.

XII.

Hail to thee, thou Only One,
Maker of these things alone !

Many are his forms of might :
Lo ! he watches thro' the night,
Ever wakeful, o'er the nation ;
Yea, and for the brute creation
Brings forth good at morning light.
Amen, Midday Sun, and thou,
Evening Sunshine, Atmu hight,
Harmachis, at morn—before thee
All the people bow,
All the people do adore thee,
Saying, " Praise with voice and song
To the god who rests among
Us whom he hath made,
Therefore homage shall be paid."

XIII.

" Hail to thee ! " all creatures cry,
Every land brings praise to thee,
From the highest height of sky
To the breadth of all the land,
To the depths of all the sea.
Yea, before thy majesty
Gods in full obedience stand ;
Bowing, at thy knees they fall
To exalt the will divine
That made them thine ;
They rejoice to meet thee,
Crying out, they greet thee,

Saying : " Father of us all,
Come in peace, for thou hast raised
Heaven, and set the earth ; therefore thou
  shalt be praised."

XIV.

Maker of all things that be,
Lord of each existing thing,
Prince of life and mortal wealth,
Body's strength and body's health,
To thee for our own creation
Gratitude and adoration
Lo ! we bring ;
And we sing,
" Praise, unto our God be praise,
For his rest upon our ways,
For his mercy all our days."

XV.

Hail to thee that makest all,
Lord of law, of gods the father ;
Mortals live but at thy call,
And the beasts that gather
Herb. Corn-bringer, thou dost give
Grass upon the thousand hills,
So the cattle live !
Hail ! all hail ! great Amen, bull,
Thou of aspect beautiful,
Karnak all thine honour fills

With the risings in thy shrine,
And at An in festival
See upon thy brow
Bright the glories shine
Of thy double coronet ;
Judge of Horus, thou
In that three days' fight with Set,*
In the giant hall.

XVI.

Chief in cycle of the gods,
One alone without compare,†
In the first of his abodes
Karnak chief, and Āni great
Whom, in circle of the gods,
First we celebrate,
Making law his daily care,
Lord of the horizon's birth,
Horus of the east.
Gold and silver without measure,
He hath hidden in the earth,
Hath created for his pleasure
Lapis lazuli of worth,

---

* The 26th day of Thoth in the old Egyptian calendar was
marked "thrice unlucky ; do nothing at all on this day ; it is
the day on which Horus fought with Set."

† *Cf.* Deut. vi. 1.

Therefore, O thou beauteous face !
Incense bring we in our hands—
Perfume from the Eastern race,
Shall be thine
When thou comest to thy feast,
Throned above the double lands,
Karnak's Lord,
And king adored,
Āni in thy shrine.

XVII.

King alone,
Of gods the One,
Many myriads are thy names—
Yea, their number is unknown :
Shining in the golden morn,
Setting in the golden west,
Every time that he is born,
Lo ! he scatters with his flames
All his enemies.
Thoth exalts his glorious eyes,
Robes him for his rest,
With the splendour of his choice ;
In his goodness gods rejoice,
For he lifteth up the heart.
Lord of the great boat,* he steers

---

* The Sekti boat.

Every dawn from out the east ;
Lord of the great boat,* that nears
Every night the west,
Travelling through the sky in rest.

XVIII.

How thy sailors cheer and shout,
Seeing Nāk, the serpent's rout,
Stabbed and slashed by knife on knife,
While the flames upon him play—
All his foul and horrid life
From his body beaten out,
And his feet cast right away.

XIX.

Then the gods lift up their voices,
Ra has slaked his soul at length,
Heliopolis is glad,
Atmu, Closer of the day,
Is victorious in the fray—
Heliopolis rejoices ;
And the Lady of our life,*
Isis, joys in heart to know
Of the serpent's overthrow,
Āpepi her good lord's foe.
Yea, the gods make salutation,

---

* The Ātet boat.   † Nebt-ānch.

Seeing Ra renew his strength :
Very low
In their shrines, with adoration,
And prostration,
See they bow.

XX.

Saved from out the serpent's jaw,
Image of the gods of law,
Thou at Karnak, by the river,
Art the lord ;
In thy name of Great Law-giver,
There thou art adored.
Lord, of sacrifice we bring
Mighty bull of offering,
In thy name of Amen, Bull,
Of his mother wonderful ;
By whose breath each man is liver,
Making all the things that are,
Or that ever came,
In thy double name,
Atmu-Cheperâ.*

XXI.

Mighty Law ! all men by thee,
Feel the joy of them that feast ;
Mighty Law ! thy gladness, see,
Lights the face and warms the breast ;

---

* Atmu, as closer of the day ; Choperâ, as creator.

Form he is of attribute
Holiest, for man or brute,
And upon his lofty brows,
Either side the royal disk,
Flies the double basilisk,
Flames and glows.
Lo, the dead in many nations
Seek unto his morn,
Turn to him the generations
Of the yet unborn,
And his glorious coming forth
Gladdens South, and gladdens North.
Hail! great Amen Ra, the lord
Of the double throne adored!
Lo! his native dwelling-place
Loves the shining of his face.

[At the end of the papyrus come these words : " Finished well as it is found." We may conclude that these are the words of the transcriber from the older papyrus.]

HYMN TO THE NILE.

NINETEENTH DYNASTY, 1400–1200 B.C.

THIS hymn is specially interesting, as being of the time of Moses, and of Israel in Egypt. The king spoken of, in verses xii. and xiv. is the king Meneptah II., son of Rameses II., who is generally considered to have been the Pharaoh of the Exodus, and who reigned between 1300 B.C. and 1266 B.C.

The author of it is well known by name. Among the literary stars that shone at the court of Meneptah— Qua-ga-bu, Hor, Merem-aput, Bek-en-ptah, Hor-a, Amon-masu, Su-an-ro, Ser-ptah—none was, in all probability, greater than the temple-scribe who wrote for the king's son, Seti II., Meneptah III., when he was still Crown Prince, the marvellous tale of " The Two Brothers." That writer was Anna, Enna, or Ennana, and was the author, also, of this famous " Hymn to the Nile."

The hymn was probably sung throughout Egypt at the great Nile festival, the " Niloa," or invocation of the blessings of the inundation, made to the tutelary deity of the Nile, " Hapi," who is represented generally on the monuments, in green and red paint, as denoting the colour of the Nile, before and at the time of inundation.

Travellers up Nile will doubtless note the three tablets of offerings, carved in the sandstone rock at Gebel Silsileh.

In the upper part of this, the king is seen making an incense-offering to the Theban triad, Amen, Mut, Khonsu, and a drink-offering to Harmachis, Ptah, Hapi. From the inscription we gather, that the Nile festivals had fallen into neglect, and that Rameses II. re-instituted the observances of the great festivals : one on the 15th of Epiphi (May 31), when the river was thought to come forth from his two chasms ; and the other on the 15th of Thoth (August 4), when the inundation arrived at Khennut, or Gebel Silsileh. The enthusiasm for Nile worship which Rameses II. felt, may be gathered from the fact, that in addition to these he, in the first year of his reign, 1333 B.C., ordained similar offerings for the solemnity that brought the ancient Nile festivals to a close, which was called the closing of the Nile book, and which took place on the 1st of Choiak (October 18).

It is thought (see Ludwig Stern's Introduction to "Ancient Festivals of the Nile," "Records of the Past," vol. x. p. 39) that the Epiphi day corresponded with the Niloa, spoken of by Heliodorus.

It seems that, in addition to this May festival of

the Nile, as ordained by Rameses II., there was one which Heliodorus heard of, as taking place a month earlier—viz., on the 15th of Payni (May 1). Early Moslem historians tell us that it was at this earlier festival, which they put at the end of April, 12th of Payni (April 28), that the Egyptians entreated the river-god for a plentiful inundation, by the sacrifice of a virgin. This festival seems to have been continued down to the time of the Arab occupation.

The Copts continued what may have been a relic of this festival, to far later times, when they cast a coffin, with a mummy's finger in it, into the river Nile.

The modern Copts still preserve a memory of this martyrs' festival in their almanac, on the 11th of Payni (April 27), called the " Lailet Nuzul en-Nuktah," when a drop is believed to fall into the Nile, and to cause its rising.*

According to Heliodorus † it was one of the principal festivals of the Egyptians. It took place about the summer solstice.

"When the river began to rise" . . . . Libanius asserts that " these rites were deemed of so much importance to the Egyptians that, unless they were performed at the proper season and in a becoming manner, by the persons appointed to this duty, they

---

* *Cf.* Lane's " Modern Egyptians," chap. xxvi.
† *Cf.* Wilkinson's " Ancient Egyptians," vol. i. chap. iv. p. 282.

felt persuaded that the Nile would refuse to rise and inundate the land. Their full belief in the efficacy of the ceremony, secured its annual performance on a grand scale. Men and women assembled, from all parts of the country, in the towns of their respective nomes. Grand festivals were proclaimed, and all the enjoyments of the table were united with the solemnity of a holy festival.

" Music, the dance, and appropriate hymns marked the respect they felt for the deity; and a wooden statue of the river-god was carried by the priests through the villages, in solemn procession, that all might appear to be honoured by his presence, while invoking the blessings he was about to confer."

According to Seneca, the priests at Philæ propitiated the deity, by throwing in offerings of gold. Be that as it may, the Nile, which begins to rise at the end of May, goes on rising till mid-October. But nowadays the principal festival, which is doubtless a relic of old times, perhaps of the festival ordered by Rameses, on the 15th day of Thoth (August 4), is the "Mósim el Khaleeg" at Cairo, in the second or third week in August, when, after the criers have gone through the city, crying the height of the Nile in the Nilometre at Rhoda, the Khedive, in the presence of State officials and a vast concourse of people who have gathered from all parts, with booths and singers, and music-makers and "fantasia," cuts the dam, and lets the

High Nile water run through the city in the old canal-bed.

As we gaze upon that motley crowd, and see the heifer slain for " Manganiyeh," or distribution of food to the people, and note the joy upon the faces of the multitude, and listen to the curious music from the players squat upon the ground, we are carried back, in thought, to the old Nile festivals of Pharaoh-days, and hear again within our ears the " Hymn to the Nile," that Ennana wrote in the time of Meneptah II.

Two copies of this hymn have been preserved to us, and may be seen at the British Museum, among the select papyri (Sallier II. p. 11, and Anastasi VII.)

The poem is interesting specially, as identifying the Nile with Ra, Amon, Ptah, and other gods, and as assuring us of the complete identification of the reigning monarch with deity, as making us realise how entirely unknown the sources of the Nile were at that day, and how the mystery of its rising affected the Egyptians with the thought of a hand unseen, that worked the yearly miracle of inundation, and gave its yearly blessing.

Readers cannot fail to note some points of resemblance to the old Hebrew poems; there are, here and there, expressions that would almost make one believe that the Hebrew Psalmist had intimate acquaintance with the works of the Egyptian hymn-writer.

Not the least remarkable passage in the hymn is

that contained in verses five and six, whence it would appear that, notwithstanding the hints of idolatrous worship throughout the poem, and the previous assertions of the hymn-writer that it is to the Nile and its inundation simply, that offerings are made and oxen slain, there is an unmistakable reference to the pure and noble worship of One God, a Supreme God, Unknown and Inconceivable, a Spirit Invisible, who " dwelleth not in temples made with hands," and for whom there is no temple that can contain him. Solomon, at his most exalted moment, breathes no more spiritual thought than Ennana here gives utterance to.

The metrical structure of the poem is also remarkable. It is divided into stanzas, containing on an average, ten couplets each. The first word of each stanza is written in red letters, each clause is brought to a close by a red point, and is made up of the same number of complete phrases. Prof. Maspero was the first to translate this religious poem, in the year 1868. Paul Guieysse has given the latest translation in the second series of " Records of the Past," vol. iii. p. 48. The prose translation, from which this metrical rendering has been made, is by the Rev. F. C. Cook (" Records of the Past," vol. iv. p. 105).

HYMN TO THE NILE.

1300–1266 B.C.

I.

HAIL, all hail, O Nile, to thee !
To this land thyself thou showest,
Coming tranquilly to give
Life, that Egypt so may live :
Ammon, hidden is thy source,
Hidden thy mysterious course,
But it fills our hearts with glee !
Thou the gardens overflowest,
With their flowers beloved of Ra ; *
Thou, for all the beasts that are,
Glorious river,
Art life-giver ;
To our fair fields ceaselessly,
Thou thy waters dost supply,
And dost come
Thro' the middle plain descending,
Like the sun thro' middle sky,
Loving good, and without ending,
Bringing corn for granary ;

---

* The sun-god was represented as delighting in flowers ; see
Ritual clxxxi.

Giving light to every home,
O thou mighty Ptah.

II.

Lord of fish, when comes the flood,
Ravening birds forsake our fields,
Maker of the spelt for food,
And of all the corn-land yields ;
He it is by whose will, stand
Strong the temples of the land.
Hater of the idle hand,
To the starving multitude
He gives labour, for the gods
Grieve in their august abodes
Over idle hands, and then
Cometh sorrow unto men.

III.

He unto the oxen's feet
Openeth all the ploughing soil,
Men with joy his coming greet.
Like to Num,* the great life-giver,
Lo he shines, and they who toil,
Very glad the whole land over,
Eat and drink beside the river ;
Every creature is in clover,
Every mouth is filled with meat.

---

* Num, the Nile-god, regarded as giver of life.

IV.

Bringing food, of plenty Lord !
All good things he doth create ;
Lord most terrible and great,
Yet of joys divine
Fount adored,
He doth in himself combine
All, and all in love doth join.
Grass to fill the oxen's mouth
He provides, to each god brings
Victims meet for offerings,
Choicest incense he supplies.
Lord of North-land, Lord of South,
He doth fill the granaries,
Wealth unto the rich man's door
Adds, and when the poor man cries,
Lo ! he careth for the poor.

V.

Growth, fulfilling all desires,
Is his law, he never tires ;
As a buckler is his might.
Not on marble is he scrolled,
Like a king with double crown ;
Him our eyes cannot behold,
Priests are needed not by him,
Offerings to him are not poured,
Not in sanctuaries dim

Is he god adored.
Yea, his dwelling is unknown,
Never yet in painted shrine,
Have we found his form divine.

VI.

There is naught we build or make *
Can our god contain.   Thy heart
Doth with no man counsel take,
Yet in thee thy youths rejoice,
And thy voice
And sovereign will
Order all their goings still.
Lo ! thy law is firm and fair
Over all the land ;
They who play the ruler's part
Are thy servants, far and near,
To command ;
North and South
Obey thy mouth,
And thy hand
Wipes from all men's eyes the tear :
Blessing is thy constant care.

VII.

Comes the glorious inundation,
Then comes joy, and then come smiles,
Hearts leap up with exultation ;
Even the jag-toothed crocodiles,

---

* 1 Kings viii. 27.

Neith's twin suckling sons, are glad,
And those gods, we count with thee,
To earth's glee
Heavenly joyance add.
Doth not Nile's outbursting flood
Overcome all men with good ?
Doth he not with his sweet waters,
Bring desire for sons and daughters?
No man's hand doth he employ,
Even without the helpful rain
He can fill our fields with grain,
And bring us mortals joy.

VIII.

In his coming from the dark land
Lo ! he giveth gleams of light ;
In the pastures, in the park-land
All he maketh with his might ;
And this river's living store
Bringeth to the birth,
Out of nothing, what on earth
Was never seen before.
Men from him their " abbas " take,
As to till his fields they fare,
Garden-plot, cucumber-square ;
For his workmen he hath care.
Evening, dewy-cold and dim,
Blazing noontide doth he make ;

Ptah and Kabes, loved of men,
Blend infinitude in him,
All within their ken
He createth—writings rare,
Sacred words—all things that are
Serviceable in the north
For the ploughman
And the bowman,
By his will he bringeth forth.

IX.

To his house he doth return,
Like a priest for oracles,
Shrinking to his urn ;
Cometh forth, just when he wills,
From his mystic fane ;
By his wrath the fish are slain,*
Then the hungry come before thee,
For the waters they implore thee,
Praying "that the Theban plain
Be like Delta, moist and green,
That each man may swift be seen
Catching up his tools, to haste
From the flood's uprising, none
Leaving fellow-men behind,
Hasting, hurrying, every one ;

---

* Lit. " Thy wrath is destruction of fishes ; " meaning that the
fish die in the pools, when the water fails.

That the nobles leave adorning,
For the waters rise,
Yea, and break up ere the morning,
Even the gods' solemnities."
So they pray; in answer comes
The refreshing water-flood,
Bringing unto all men food
And fatness for their homes.

X.

Thou who dost the judgment-seat
Firm establish; men rejoice,
Flattering thee with grateful voice;
Worshippers thy coming greet,
Thee, their lord,
With thy mighty waters poured.
Unto thee, with praise, they bring
Gifts of corn for offering,
When the gods are all adored;
For no fowls upon the land
Fall when thou art by.
Gold they give thee for thy hand,
Gold, in ingots moulded pure,
Gifts of lapis lazuli,
So, secure
The corn shall lie—
So, no hungry bird shall eat
The germinating wheat.

XI.

Hymns to thee the harper plays,
Playing with a skilful hand;
All thy youths for thee are glad,
Children they, thine own.
Thou with full reward dost crown
Their laborious days,
Thou the mighty one, to add
Fit adorning to the land;
And they feel thy great enlightening,
When thou sendest from above
Flashings of thy silver shield;
Then their hearts, with joy, are brightening,
For they know that thou dost love
All the increase of the field.

XII.

In the city of the king*
Thou dost shine;
Then the householder may dine,
Faring on each dainty thing.
He who gnawed the lotus-root †
When the food was scant,
Laughs at such a pauper's fare;

---

* Probably Thebes is the city alluded to, and the king is Meneptah II., son of Rameses II.

† Lit. "The poor man laughs at the lotus" which he ate when, in time of scarcity, he could get nothing better.

Perfectly thou dost prepare
All things that thy children want,
Orderest every herb and fruit ;
But if food, from out thy hand,
Fail, then joyance too must fail ;
Hearts are weary, cheeks are pale
In a weary land.

XIII.

River ! when thy waters rise,
Offerings unto thee we make,
Oxen unto thee we slay,
For thee keep our holiday,
Fowls to thee we sacrifice,
Beasts for thee the hunters take,
And unto thy holy name
Rise the gifts of purest flame ;
Unto all the gods that be,
Do we bring
An offering,
When we sacrifice to thee.
Incense-clouds ascend to heaven,
Oxen, bulls, and fowls are given
To thine altar's fiery mouth,
When from out the double cave*—

---

* An allusion to the Egyptian tradition that the Nile issues
from two chasms or openings, in the south. Perhaps at that time
the sources of the Blue and White Nile were known.

Those two openings in the south—
Comes the mighty river,
Nile, of name, in heaven unknown,
Nile, whose forms are never shown
Forms no man hath sculptured ever,
None can paint or grave.

XIV.

Men extol him, and the gods
Praise him in their high abodes;
Yea, each great and terrible one
Stands in awe of him;
And his son the king, is given,
Lord of all,* to send from heaven
Light to Egypt dim,
Light to Egypt, south and north.
Wherefore, river, shine thou forth!
Rise and shine! upon us smile!
Thou who givest life, by giving
Oxen, for the ploughman's team,
Thou who for the oxen's living,
Makest pasture by the stream,
Shine upon us, glorious Nile!

---

* The Pharaoh is spoken of here as the son of the Nile, and
a delicate hint of his divine sonship to the god Ra, in his office
of enlightener, is made at one and the same time.

LAMENTATIONS OF ISIS AND NEPHTHYS.

PTOLEMAIC DYNASTY, 305–27 B.C.

No one interested in the art of working in hard stone, but will look with interest on the beautiful group of black serpentine figures, now in the Bûlâk Museum, which Mariette Bey brought from the tomb at Sakkarah, of a certain high functionary of the Saitic Court, Psamtik by name, who, we may suppose, lived about 600 years B.C. The group consists of a magnificently modelled Hathor, in form of a cow, protecting the defunct, in Amenti. Right and left sit, on separate thrones, Osiris and Isis—the former with the crook and scourge of office, the latter with the key of life upon her lap—and if we are impressed by the tender kindness of the face of Hathor, beaming above the deceased who puts his trust in her, we are certainly as much struck by the beneficence upon the faces both of Isis and Osiris. However much Pantheism led to animal worship and materialism in later times, it is, I think, plain that Psamtik, who lived, it must be remembered, in the twenty-sixth dynasty, that gave such honour to the cult of Apis, did, nevertheless, believe in the spiritual powers of love and life and light that could not die, and in a judge of merciful loving-kindness in the world beyond. Turning from these monuments to a little stele of limestone, which I dare to call the stele of the shrine of the Resurrection, one sees Osiris, standing erect, and looking certainly less benign, and above his head may be noticed a full sun's disk with a scarabæus right upon it, and on either side, upon bended knee, a dog-faced ape, sacred to Thoth, and ever present above the scales of right and wrong in the Hall of Judgment, bending in adoration. What can all this mean, but that Osiris is not only Judge, but also Lord of the Resurrection of the Just?

Travellers in Egypt who remember what the hope of the resurrection and the belief in a Saviour of the living, who is also a Judge of the dead, has been to the last nineteen centuries of Christendom, will stand in reverence before the thought of what a kindred hope —like, but how unlike—effected for thrice that number of centuries, in the valley of the Nile.

A belief in an Osiris who, as Plutarch says, "takes pleasure in doing good," and whose name, amongst many other meanings, was said to denote activity and beneficence—a belief in an Osiris who came on earth as the benefactor of mankind, who was put to death, and who rose again, and who sits in the hall of judgment to judge the spirits of all the departed, was the sheet-anchor of the faith of old Egypt. To this belief in a resurrection, the monuments, from the oldest pyramid to the latest Ptolemaic and Roman temple, bear witness; and as we Christians have our Holy Sepulchre, so the Egyptians had theirs. The head of Osiris, when it was found at last, was reverentially buried at Abȳdos; and, whether we are right in iden-tifying ancient This with Abȳdos, or with Girgeh, a few miles to the north, it is pretty certain that round that sacred tomb of Osiris, there had grown such a cult, that all the glory of Chufu (of the fourth dynasty) was unable, with his temple at Denderah, to attract either commerce or people away from that sacred spot where the head of Osiris was buried.

Over the holy sepulchre grew, for hundreds of years, an ever-increasing mound of tombs. That mound, known to us to-day as Kom es Sultân, at Abȳdos, has been carefully excavated. Sixth, twelfth, and thir-teenth dynasty tombs, roughly speaking from 3700 B.C. to 2800 B.C., abound. It is believed there are earlier tombs, and there certainly were later ones. Plutarch tells us that wealthy inhabitants were brought from all parts of Egypt to be interred at Abȳdos, in order that they might repose close to Osiris. At what date the cult of Osiris rose, or became separate from the cult of Ra, we cannot know, but it is in the nature of things that the humanity and personality demanded of their presiding deities by the worshippers, turned after a time from the far-off Ra in his golden boat, passing each day to battle with Āpepi, the dragon of

Q

cloud and darkness and all evil, to the more tangible form of the same teaching in the person of Osiris. That the cult of Osiris is of later date than the cult of Ra, may be inferred from a passage in the " Book of the Dead," as quoted by Page Renouf, which says that " Osiris came to Tattu (Mendes) and found the soul of Ra there." It would appear that the later cult became from that time entirely one with the earlier, for the passage concludes thus—" each embraced the other, and became as one soul in two souls." How late the cult of Osiris lingered on in Egypt one learns best at Philæ. Philæ owes all its beauty of temple-building to the fact that it was looked upon as another of the holy sepulchres of Osiris—an oath sworn by Osiris of Philæ could not be broken—and from one of the Greek laudatory inscriptions on the first pylon of the Temple of Isis there, written by pilgrims to the shrine, we learn that there, so late as A.D. 453, under the Emperor Martian, and seventy years after the proclamation of the famous Edict of Theodosius against the religion of old Egypt, there still lived in that holy island, priests who celebrated the rites of Isis and Osiris.

The visitor to the Romanic-Egyptian Temple of Denderah, if he passes by the little Iseium at the N.W. end of the temple, will see a pylon hard by, which was dedicated to Isis in the thirty-first year of Cæsar Augustus.

Jesus Christ was then four years old, and those of us who enter that temple and visit the chambers of the invocation of Isis, and of Osiris, restored to strength, and power over death—of Osiris risen again—chambers which lie immediately to the south of the central shrine of the golden barks, will remember that it is probable that the sculpturing of this resurrection story did not take place till the teaching of Christ on the resurrection of the dead, had already begun to sound in Egypt.

The cult of Osiris was universal. Ammon might be worshipped at Thebes, Ptah at Memphis, Sutek at San, Horus at Heliopolis, Khnoum at Elephantiné; but Osiris was worshipped universally.

Egypt was divided into forty-two provinces, and in addition to the universal or principal Osiris, each of these provinces worshipped a local Osiris also. One did not realise this till one passed on to the roof of the temple at Denderah, and there entered the little temple, with its two groups of chambers, dedicated to the Osiris of Denderah, under the title of Osiris-An. At a glance one saw that the six chambers of the temple were divided into two sets. To the three on the north, the worshipper of the Osiris of the northern provinces had access; and the three chambers of the south were dedicated to the Osiris gods of the southern provinces.

There on the walls were seen, not local, but national

traditions of the Osiris, under his forty-two names for the forty-two nomes, or provinces. Long processions of gods were there seen, carrying in their vases the limbs of Osiris, which each town possessed, and there, too, were portrayed the forty-two funeral biers of the good god.

The traveller who visits Denderah, comes away with the impression that the Romans and Egyptians, who, upon Ptolemaic foundations, were intending to build a temple to Venus, finished by building a temple to the True and Beautiful and Good, and to their sure and certain hope of a joyful resurrection of these three powers that are immortal.

But he will be much impressed by the permanence and vitality of the cult of Osiris, which, in the decadence of fortune and religion, could so appeal to the heart of Alexandrian, Greek, Roman, and Egyptian, as to bring it about that the latest monuments of the land should be teachers of the truths of Osiris, and witnesses for a faith in a resurrection.

As I stood one day in that most interesting of Hypethral chapels—the chapel of the bringing together of the limbs of Osiris—on the roof of the Temple of Philæ—I heard a young English girl say to her father: "I can't make it out, the guide-book says that Isis was the sister, as well as the wife of Osiris."

"Nonsense, my dear, the thing's impossible. I never heard such a thing in my life."

An American stepped forward, and said to me: "Wall sir, ken you tell me whether it was Isis or Osiris that was Mr.? I've got rather mixed."

It may, perhaps, be of service, then, to travellers up Nile, to have in brief the legend of a cult so universal and so indelibly impressed upon old Egypt, that the very arms of the river Nile in the Delta, or, as they called it, "legs of the river," were thought of only as another form of the good god Osiris.

We will premise that Osiris is the personification of the eternal antagonism of good and evil, light and darkness, life and death.

Osiris, smitten by the genius of evil, Typhon, dies, but rises again, again to fall, again to rise undyingly. Osiris is the eldest of the five children of Seb and Nut. He is greater than his father, more powerful than his mother ; while yet in his mother's womb he weds his sister Isis, and their offspring was the elder Horus. Set and Nephthys are their brother and sister, who also marry one another. Osiris is attacked by Set, and slain, but is avenged by Horus, his son, and reigns as judge of the dead in the Hall of the two-fold Right.

But if one should wish for a fuller account of the legend, one had better go to the pseudo-Plutarch, " De Iside et Osiride " xii–xx. There one may find, interwoven with mysticism, a carefully written account of the story of Isis and Osiris, as it was current at the end of the first century of the Christian era.

The gods, tired of reigning in heaven, began to reign upon earth by turns, in the likeness of men. Osiris was fifth king and lord of Egypt, north and south. His reign was beneficent. He brought the country from barbarism and poverty to law and order, to wealth, to reverence and worship. He taught the people agriculture and the art of music. In a temporary absence from his kingdom, Isis, his queen, took the government. Typhon Suteckh, or Set, determined to overthrow Osiris, but Isis was too vigilant for him. On the return of Osiris, Typhon, who had taken the measure of Osiris' body, caused a beautiful chest to be made, and at a banquet, given in Osiris' honour, promised the chest to any one who, lying down in it, should find it fit him.

Of course the company all try, but it fits none but Osiris. He lies down in it, in a trice the conspirators, who are in the secret, clap the lid down, fasten it, and carry it away to the sea by the Tanaitic mouth of the Nile, which was ever afterwards held to be accursed.

When Isis hears of it, she is disconsolate, and goes forth mourning, in search of the chest. Nephthys, her sister, accompanies her. She hears of it as being washed ashore in the papyrus swamp of the Syrian Byblos.

She goes thither, finds that the chest had lodged in a

tamarisk tree—the tamarisk had grown, and completely enveloped it, had been cut down and become a pillar of the king's house.

For her service to the Queen and Court ladies, with whom she ingratiated herself as a kind of lady's maid, she obtained permission to cut the chest from out of the tamarisk pillar, and having secured it, sailed away for Egypt, opened the chest upon a desert shore, laid her face upon her husband's, put her arms about his dead body, and made lamentation. She had determined to bury Osiris, after embalmment, at Memphis, but on a moonlight night, Typhon, out hunting, came upon it, and recognising the body, tore it into fourteen pieces, and some say, scattered them up and down the country. Isis again sets out to seek the fragments in a papyrus boat, for which reason the crocodiles refuse to touch people who sail in such vessels.

After these things, Osiris, returning from the other world, appeared to his son Horus, urged him to battle against Typhon, and instructed him in the use of arms.

In a pitched battle which lasted many days, Horus was victor, and Typhon, or Set, was taken prisoner. He was sent in chains to Isis, but she, instead of slaying him, loosed his chains and set him, her own brother, free. Horus, mad with indignation, laid hands on his mother Isis, tore off her crown, or, as some say, struck off her head, and in place of it, to repair the injury, Thoth gave her a cow's head and horns. After this Horus renewed the battle with his uncle Set, or Typhon, and slew him with a long spear, which he drove into his head.

Now for the explanation of the myth. The parents of Osiris, we remember, were Earth and Heaven, Seb and Nut. The Earth being looked upon as Father of all, and Heaven as Mother. Travellers may see Nut constantly represented as bending her star-spangled body over the whole earth, nowhere better than on the lids of the sarcophagi in the Gizeh Museum and in the ceiling of the Court of Heaven, of the Temple of Denderah. And wherever they see a man, with a goose standing upon his head, they may know that they are looking upon a representative of the earth, to whom the goose was dedicated; Seb being looked upon as the great cackler who laid the egg of the earth and hatched it. From the marriage of Earth and Heaven, Seb and Nut, sprang Osiris the Sun, and Isis the Dawn. Joined in wedlock before they issued from their mother's womb, they two had a son— Horus, this was the Sun in his full strength. The kingdom of Osiris was the sunrise. The destroyer of the sunrise is Darkness (Set) who, with his spouse, the Sunset (Nephthys), reigns in the West. Nephthys also has a child, some say by Osiris; that child is Anubis the Dusk. The victory of Set, or Typhon, over Isiris is a victory of Darkness over Light, Night over Day, and the resurrection of Osiris is the rising of the Sun.

For how many ages the sun had risen and set before men saw in his beneficent coming, a kindly father of their spirits, and in his going, need for lamentation and tears; for how many years the light of day had been swallowed up in darkness before men felt, within their hearts, that it spoke to them of a daily struggle of evil against good ; for how many years they saw the triumphant sunrise, before day by day it spoke to them of the certain triumph of good over evil, and the faith of a resurrection to eternal life beyond the grave, found echo within their souls, we know not. This we know, that one, at any rate, of the two races that lie buried side by side in the third dynasty mounds, by the " pyramid of the rising," at Mêdûm, must have felt that there was a mysterious union between their chance of another life, and the certain rising of the god of morn.

Those of us who pass up the Osirian river towards the temple, where the latest rites of the god were held inviolate, and who witness, as old Egypt witnessed, the rising of the day-star in scarlet and fine linen over the eastern cliffs ; his golden-crowned glory at noon, and his death in the sea of blood above the purple desert to the west, may well be awed by the thought of to how many millions of minds, for how many thousands of years, in this valley of the Nile, the daily triumph of the Osirian god, and mighty tragedy of his death, brought comfort and sorrow.

It was my fortune, as I descended from the shattered, but gigantic funeral mound of Kom es Sultân, to see a dead man carried to burial with Mahommedan rites.

The lamentation of Isis was in my ears, and I felt that the legend of Osiris had probably brought, to every grave in ancient Egypt, more of consolation than is often felt at a moslem grave in modern Egypt. For, once a year at least (at the Feast of Osiris for the dead), in those old times the dead man's friends seem to have come to the temple, and there, through the lips of priests and priestesses, coupled the names of their dead with Osiris, and invoked them, as already endowed, with the great god's life, and already enjoying the blessing of his fellowship ; and back would return from the temple gates, with as sure and certain a hope of the joyful resurrection of the departed, as of the sun's rising in the morning. It is not too much to ask the traveller in Egypt, if he should be at Denderah on some 13th day of November, to imagine that, though he hears not the sound of any zither or pipes—for these were forbidden in the commencement of Osirian festivals—he may still see two beautiful priestesses "beautiful in all their members" seated at the principal door of the hall where the judgment scene is painted ; and whilst he notes the Memphian bread in one hand, and the crystal vase of water in the other, he may hear from their lips arise the passionate prayer to Osiris-An :—" Come to thine abode, oh come to thine abode, excellent sovereign, come to thine abode."

The papyrus, probably of about the time of the Ptolemies, from which the accompanying lamentation of Isis and Nephthys is taken, was found at Thebes, inside a statue, representing Osiris, by M. Passalaqua. It is now in the Royal Museum, Berlin ; partially translated by H. Brugsch in 1852, it has since been entirely translated by M. P. I. de Horrack. It has analogy with the Book of Respirations, and the Book of Glorifying Isis, which, in later Egyptian times, seem to have superseded the Book of the Dead. It repre- sents Isis and Nephthys making lamentation and prayers, to effect the resurrection of their brother Osiris, and, from the fact that the name of a certain Tentrut is joined with Osiris in the opening recital, it is certain that the resurrection of the dead man is also kept in mind by the reciting women who personified the sisters of Osiris, at the time of the solemnities on the 25th day of Choiak,* at the third and eighth hours of the day.†

---

* Choiak commenced Oct. 18.

† This metrical rendering is based on M. de Horrack's trans- lation, " Records of the Past," vol. ii. p. 119.

THE LAMENTATION OF ISIS AND NEPHTHYS.

305–27 B.C.

RECITAL of the potent formulæ
Made by the two, the sisters, the divine,
Isis and Nephthys, in the house of god
Osiris, he who liveth in the west,
Lord of Abȳdos; the recitals made
In the month Choiak, day the twenty-fifth.
Where'er Osiris doth abide, the same
Recited are, in all his festivals,
And they are beneficial to his soul,
Make firm his body, and diffuse a joy
Through all his being; to his nostrils give
Breath, and sweet coolness to his parchèd throat;
Isis and Nephthys' heart they satisfy,
Place Horus on the throne-seat of his father,
Give life, stability, tranquillity
To Osiris-Tentrut, born of Takha-aa,
Surnamed Persais, he the justified,
And to recite them it is profitable,
Conformably with words that are divine.

EVOCATION BY ISIS.

To thine abode, to thine abode, oh come,
To thine abode, god An, I thee implore,
Thine enemies exist not any more;
Return, oh glorious sovereign, to thine home.

I am thy sister, whom thou hast embraced,
Look on me, I, thy sister, loving thee;
Oh, beauteous youth, stay not thou far from me,
But come to thine abode with haste, with haste.

I see thee not, and to my heart doth throng
Anguish for thee, and bitterness untold;
Mine eyes seek to thee, wishing to behold—
Ere I behold will it be long, be long?

How long, oh glorious sovereign, must I yearn,
Before the sight of thee mine eyes shall bless?
God An, beholding thee is happiness,
To her who loveth thee, return, return.

Oh, Un-nefer,* the justified in state,
Come to thy sister, come unto thy wife,
Oh, Urt-het,* lo, one mother gave us life,
Thyself from me no longer separate.

---

* Un-nefer and Urt-het are surnames of Osiris.

The gods and men towards thee turn their faces,
Weeping for thee when they behold my tears.
I make lament, but there is none that hears,
Yea, though with plaint, unto the heavenly places,
I, who so loved thee here on earth, do cry,
Thy sister, none hath loved thee more than I.

EVOCATION OF NEPHTHYS.

OH sovereign most excelling,
Come now unto thy dwelling,
Rejoice, for all thine enemies are dead ;
Thy sisters twain around thy funeral-bed,
Their guardian watch are keeping,
And call on thee with weeping,
Whose limbs upon the lion-couch are spread.

Our tender, sweet solicitude thou seest, speak a word ;
Speak, supreme one, mighty Ruler, Lord and King.
Chase away the pain that now our hearts doth wring :
Gods and men, thy company,
When they see thee, lo, they cry
Look upon us, oh supreme one, ruler, Lord—

It is life for us thy face to contemplate,
Let thy face be turned away
From us never more, we pray,
For the joy of our heart's being
Is to see thee, and in seeing,
Oh, sovereign, our heart's happiness is great.

I am Nephthys, I thy sister, I who love thee,
Thy foe is vanquishèd,

He lives not, he is dead.
I am near thee, and for ever
Those limbs they did dissever,
Protecting them from harm, I bend above thee.

Here follow two invocations to Osiris, under the forms of the moon and the sun, expressing the joy of his two sisters, Isis and Nephthys, at having thus perceived him. The lamentation concludes with an invocation by Isis, of which a translation is given.

INVOCATION BY ISIS.

OH come to thine abode, into thy dwelling,
To thine abode return, oh ! King excelling.

Come and behold, to thy son Horus given,
The sovereign-rule supreme of earth and heaven.

Cities he hath and districts at desire,
By that respect his greatness doth inspire.

Of him the heaven and earth are both in awe,
The far barbarians tremble at his law.

Lo, thy companions who are men and gods
Have become his, in the divine abodes.

In either hemisphere they do his will,
And all thy rites they faithfully fulfil.

These two are near thee now, the sisters thine,
Pouring libations to thy form divine.

Horus, thy son, for funeral offering
Doth bread and beverage, geese and oxen bring.

Thoth chanteth to thee songs of festival,
By his good formulæ on thee doth call.

The sons of Horus keep thy members whole,
And every day they benefit thy soul.

Horus, thy son, salutes thee in thy shrine,
And gives thee things, by consecration thine.

In hand behold the gods their vases take,
And to thy being, their libations make.

Ruler supreme, our Lord, we thee implore,
From thy companions be not absent more.

———

The place where this recital goeth forward
Is very holy, let none see or hear,
Save the head priest who reads the panegyrics,
And he who doth preside o'er rituals.
First, are two women, beautiful of form,
Brought in and made to sit upon the ground,
There, at the great door of the Hall of Judgment.
And then the names of Isis and of Nephthys
Are written on their shoulders.   Crystal jars
Of water, next are placed in their right hands,
And in their left hands, loaves of Memphian bread.
Let them see all the ritual rightly done,
Both at the third and eighth hour of the day,
And at the hour of the ceremony,
Cease not the recitation of this book.

(It is finished.)

LAMENT OF THE DEAD WIFE OF PASHERENPTAH.

PTOLEMAIC DYNASTY, 305–27 B.C.

NOTWITHSTANDING the fact that, during the Ptolemaic Renaissance, there seems to have been a greater prominence given to the worship of Osiris, and a more passionate appeal than ever to the hearts of men, to see in the sunrise a new birth for the hope of the Resurrection of the Dead, there were minds to which this teaching brought no comfort; it would almost appear that something of the early Egyptian belief in the condition of happiness beyond the tomb, had lost its hold on the hearts of men.

Upon this phase of declining belief, the following sorrowful lament from the grave, from one of the latest Ptolemaic tablets, and reproduced in Sharpe's " Egyptian Inscriptions," i. pl. 4, is a sad commentary. Readers who compare this cry from Hades, of the dead wife to her beloved husband, with the " Funeral Dirge of King Antef," or the " Song of the Harper," will see that, at any rate in those earlier times, though the dead men bade their living brothers enjoy life while they might, they always suggested that it would be well to bear in mind that death came, and after death came judgment, and that for the deeds done well in the body here, there would be a happier life in the world of spirit.

But this cry of the dead wife is more bitter than the wail of the Greek hero: " Better it is to be a slave on earth, than a king in Hades."

There is a note of hopeless sadness about it, of un-ending gloom and sorrowful separation from all one's kin, and all love, and all that made life worth living, which is tragic in its pathos. " Death Absolute " has seldom had the thickness of his black darkness put forth more plaintively.

Pasherenptah loved his wife, and she had borne him, we read, " handsome girls," but he was now forty-three years old, and as yet, he had no son. He had prayed to the God I-em-hotep for a son " to re-main in his place for ever, and ever to keep alive the name of his house." The prayer had been granted, and it is allowable for us to read between the lines of his wife's lamentation in Hades, and to believe that she was passionately attached to a very tender hus-band and a beloved child. That she had spoiled her husband, and let him have his own way in everything, is, I think, also apparent from the context; but the devotion to him, her wish in her abode of darkness and sorrow that he and his house should be full of sunshine and joy, is most touching.   The picture of the utter helplessness of the dead, is terribly graphic.

The prose translation of which this metrical rendering is given, will be found in Page Renouf's "Hibbert Lectures," p. 242.   References to the tablet of Pasherenptah will be found pp. 141, 156.

LAMENT OF THE DEAD WIFE OF
PASHERENPTAH.

305–27 B.C.

BROTHER and spouse of mine,
Cease not to drink the wine
  And cup of gladness.
Love women while you may,
Make life one holiday,
Keep all thy care away,
  Banish earth's sadness.

For, in Amenti, all
Feel darkness like a pall,
  Heavy as sorrow.
Here in the land of sleep,
Each his own place must keep,
Wrapped in a slumber deep
  That knows no morrow.

Ah! and the bitter pain,
Never to see again
  Sister or brother;

Never to feel the heart,
For wife and child to start,
Never to recognise
　　Father and mother.

You, underneath the sun,
Where living waters run,
　　Drink, but I drink not;
For you sweet waters flow
I cannot taste, nor know
Since I came, where I am,
　　See not, and think not.

I for the streams that pass
By me, must cry, "Alas,"
　　My lips not steeping;
Yea, for the pleasant breeze
There, in the river-trees,
That so my sorrow cease,
　　Still am I weeping.

"Absolute Death" is god
Here, in this dread abode,
　　Death! none adore him.
All men obey his call,
Yea, and he cries to all,
Down on their knees they fall,
　　Trembling before him.

Death ! no respecter he
Of person or degree,
    In earth or heaven ;
Treats all alike, none pray,
He hears not what they say;
Takes not, on festal day,
    Offerings given.

THE HEROIC POEM OF PEN-TA-UR.*

NINETEENTH DYNASTY, 1400–1200 B.C.

VISITORS at Thebes, to the Memnonium, or the tomb of Osymandyas, better known as the Ramesseum, will never forget two things—one the " shattered visage " of stone, of which an English poet has sung; the other the great battle-scene upon both pylons, which the Egyptian poet has immortalised.

The following translation is a fragment of this heroic poem of the Nineteenth Dynasty, the most remarkable epic poem in Egyptian history.

Its author was a not very reputable court-poet named Pen-ta-ur who, two years after the battle he describes, namely, in the seventh year of Rameses II. 1326 B.C., won for his prize-poem the glory of having it made a national epic, to be inscribed with illustrations, upon the temple walls, and for himself a deathless immortality. The text of the poem, written in honour of Rameses' prowess in single combat against the Khita, was, by command of the King,

---

* The name is also spelt Pentaour, and by more recent scholars Pen-ta-urt.

inscribed upon the walls of the temples of Abȳdos, Luxor, Karnak, the Ramesseum and Ibsambûl. By their enormous illustrations on the temple-walls and pylons, the sculptors seem to have vied with its author, to make the poem a permanent possession of the people.

He who turns his back upon the northern pylon at Luxor to pass down the great Sphinx-dromos which is now being unearthed, and so to Karnak, must feel that that way was really in old time, a triumphal way of the poem of Pen-ta-ur. For, there on the Luxor pylon, is the poem pictured, and it will be in his mind all the way, till he enters the main south gate, at the eastern end of the great Hall of Columns, and lo, when entering, there on the left hand side, upon the wall, the text of the poem is written plain.

But it is at the Ramesseum, if he is fortunate in obtaining a good light, that he will best understand the situations that the poem describes. Had no poem been written, those sculptures, with their tale of camp life and battle, in the time of Rameses the King, would be well worth going all the way from England to see.

As I write, I can hardly help smiling at the way in which his friends, the Hittites of Kadesh, who had come to the rescue of the poor King of Aleppo, are tilting him up to let the water drain out of him, after his unlucky bath in the river Orontes. The pictures are as real as they are humorous.

Mariette Bey * may well be quoted at length here: "The scene is laid in Syria, on the banks of a river which everything seems to point out as the Orontes. Rameses is present in person, and comes fully armed, to dispute possession of the country, designated under the generic name of the Khetas. Kadesh is the nearest town. Through a concourse of circumstances, which do not reflect credit on the Egyptian generals, Rameses finds himself surrounded by his enemies. The soldiers who formed the escort, have taken flight. Rameses stands alone, and no one is with him."

With unreflecting valour, he throws himself among the chariots. He kills the chiefs of the "vile Khetas," forces their troops to recross the river in hot haste, and by personal courage, turns the threatened rout into a complete victory. This brilliant feat of arms is what the first pylon of the Ramesseum commemorates.

On one side, Rameses is seen precipitating himself into the thickest of the fight. The enemy fly in terror; some are crushed under the feet of the horses and under the chariot-wheels; some lie dead on the ground, pierced with arrows, shot by the king's own hand; others again leap into the river and are drowned. On the opposite side the king is represented seated on his throne, his officers come forward

---

* "Monuments of Upper Egypt," p. 191.

tendering their congratulations ; but it is with reproofs
the king receives them. " Not one among you," he
exclaims, " has behaved well in thus deserting me,
and leaving me alone in the midst of the enemy. The
princes and the captains did not join hands with me
in fight. I have put to flight thousands of nations,
and I was all alone."

On the interior façade of the second pylon, one may
see, by the evening light, the same king in the thick of
the battle. Here Grabatousa, the armour-bearer of the
Prince of the Khita, falls pierced by the arrows of the
king ; there Rabsounna, captain of the archers, meets
with the same fate. The Orontes lies in the path of
the Khita, who fly in disorder. Upon one of the
pylons, one notices the square camp of the Egyptians,
surrounded by its wall of shields, which the
Egyptian warriors have placed around it. The life of
the camp servants, resting by their baggage, comes
before us. The asses, some of them giving a little
trouble, are loose within the enclosure. Pharaoh's
tent is seen in the midst of the camp. The favourite
lion, " Tearer-in-pieces," stalks about, and near it is the
shrine of the great gods of Egypt. When one reads
the poem of Pen-ta-ur, one realises that all this
last picture represents the encampment of the first
legion of Ammon, the body-guard of the king, that
gave way so disastrously on the great day of battle.

Another wall-sculpture gives us a spirited picture of

the battle, at the critical moment of Rameses' single-handed victory. The river Orontes runs round two sides of the picture, and the flight of the Hittites' horses and chariots towards the stream, the falling into it of the pursued, " as crocodiles fall into the water," is graphically portrayed. A copy of this battle-scene is given in Ebers' " Egypt," vol. ii. p. 279.

The papyrus from which this poem was originally translated, is known as the third Sallier papyrus, one of several that were purchased from an Egyptian sailor, by M. Sallier of Aix, in Provence. It is now in the British Museum. It is a copy of an earlier document. It was seen by Champollion in 1833, but to Vicomte de Rouget belongs the credit of having first attempted a full translation of it, in the year 1856.

Mr. Goodwin translated it in 1858, and Professor Lushington's translation of it is given in vol. ii. of " Records of the Past," p. 65.

Henry Brugsch Bey, after comparing the various texts of the poem on the monuments, and papyri fragments, and having carefully studied the well-known papyrus of the British Museum, has produced a very full translation, a portion of which is here metrically rendered.

Readers should compare Brugsch Bey's translation (" History of the Pharaohs," vol. ii. p. 53) with that of Professor Lushington.

THE HEROIC POEM OF PEN-TA-UR.

1326 B.C.

RELATING THE VICTORY OF RAMESES II. OVER THE
KHITA, 1328 B.C.

THEN the king of Khita-land,
With his warriors made a stand,
But he durst not risk his hand
In battle with our Pharaoh;
So his chariots drew away,
Unnumbered as the sand,
And they stood, three men of war
On each car;
And gathered all in force
Was the flower of his army, for the fight in full array,
But advance, he did not dare,
Foot or horse.

So in ambush there they lay,
North-west of Kadesh town;
And while these were in their lair,

Others went forth south of Kadesh, on our midst, their
    charge was thrown
With such weight, our men went down,
For they took us unaware,
And the legion of Pra-Hormakhu gave way.

But at the western side
Of Arunatha's tide,
Near the city's northern wall, our Pharaoh had his
    place.
And they came unto the king,
And they told him our disgrace;
Then Rameses uprose, like his father,* Month, in
    might,
All his weapons took in hand,
And his armour did he don,
Just like Baal, fit for fight;
And the noble pair of horses that carried Pharaoh on,
Lo! "Victory of Thebes" was their name,
And from out the royal stables of great Miamun they
    came.

Then the king he lashed each horse,
And they quickened up their course,

---

* Month, or Mentu, as one of the aspects of the sun-god Ra,
was worshipped at Thebes.

And he dashed into the middle of the hostile, Hittite
    host,
All alone, none other with him, for he counted not
    the cost.
Then he looked behind, and found
That the foe were all around,
Two thousand and five hundred of their chariots of
    war ;
And the flower of the Hittites, and their helpers, in a
    ring—
Men of Masu, Keshkesh, Pidasa, Malunna, Arathu,
Qazauadana, Kadesh, Akerith, Leka and Khilibu—
Cut off the way behind,
Retreat he could not find ;
There were three men on each car,
And they gathered all together, and closed upon the
    king.
"Yea, and not one of my princes, of my chief men
    and my great,
Was with me, not a captain, not a knight ;
For my warriors and chariots had left me to my fate,
Not one was there to take his part in fight."

Then spake Pharaoh, and he cried : " Father Ammon,
    where art thou ?
Shall a sire forget his son ?

Is there aught without thy knowledge I have done?
From the judgments of thy mouth when have I gone?
Have I e'er transgressed thy word?
Disobeyed, or broke a vow?
Is it right, who rules in Egypt, Egypt's lord,
Should e'er before the foreign peoples bow,
Or own their rod?
Whate'er may be the mind of this Hittite herdsman-
    horde,
Sure Ammon * should stand higher than the wretch
    who knows no God?
Father Ammon is it nought
That to thee I dedicated noble monuments, and filled
Thy temples with the prisoners of war?
That for thee a thousand years shall stand the shrines
    I dared to build?
That to thee my palace-substance I have brought,
That tribute unto thee from afar
A whole land comes to pay,
That to thee ten thousand oxen for sacrifice I fell,
And burn upon thine altars the sweetest woods that
    smell;
That all thy heart required, my hand did ne'er gainsay.
I have built for thee tall gatesand wondrous works,
    beside the Nile,
I have raised thee mast on mast,
For eternity to last,

---

* The king, probably, is here identifying himself with Ammon.

S

From Elephantin's isle
The obelisks for thee I have conveyed,
It is I who brought alone
The everlasting stone,
It is I who sent for thee,
The ships upon the sea,
To pour into thy coffers the wealth of foreign trade ;
Is it told that such a thing
By any other king,
At any other time, was done at all ?
Let the wretch be put to shame
Who refuses thy commands,
But honour to his name
Who to Ammon lifts his hands.
To the full of my endeavour,
With a willing heart for ever,
I have acted unto thee,
And to thee great God I call ;
For behold ! now Ammon, I,
In the midst of many peoples, all unknown,
Unnumbered as the sand,
Here I stand,
All alone ;
There is no one at my side,
My warriors and chariots afeared,
Have deserted me, none heard
My voice, when to the cravens I, their king, for
    succour, cried.

But I find that Ammon's grace
Is better far to me
Than a million fighting men and ten thousand chariots
    be.
Yea, better than ten thousand, be they brother, be
    they son,
When with hearts that beat like one,
Together for to help me they are gathered in one
    place.
The might of men is nothing, it is Ammon who is
    lord,
What has happened here to me is according to thy
    word,
And I will not now transgress thy command ;
But alone, as here I stand,
To thee my cry I send,
Unto earth's extremest end,
Saying, " Help me, father Ammon, against the Hittite
    horde."

Then my voice it found an echo in Hermonthis'
    temple-hall,
Ammon heard it, and he came unto my call ;
And for joy I gave a shout,
From behind, his voice cried out,
" I have hastened to thee, Ramses Miamun,

Behold ! I stand with thee,
Behold ! 'tis I am he,
Own father thine, the great god Ra, the sun.
Lo ! mine hand with thine shall fight,
And mine arm is strong above
The hundreds of ten thousands, who against thee do
    unite,
Of victory am I lord, and the brave heart do I love,
I have found in thee a spirit that is right,
And my soul it doth rejoice in thy valour and thy
    might.

Then all this came to pass, I was changèd in my heart
Like Monthu, god of war, was I made,
With my left hand hurled the dart,
With my right I swung the blade,
Fierce as Baal in his time, before their sight.
Two thousand and five hundred pairs of horses were
    around,
And I flew into the middle of their ring,
By my horse-hoofs they were dashed all in pieces to
    the ground,
None raised his hand in fight,
For the courage in their breasts had sunken quite ;
And their limbs were loosed for fear,
And they could not hurl the dart,

And they had not any heart
To use the spear ;
And I cast them to the water,
Just as crocodiles fall in from the bank,
So they sank.
And they tumbled on their faces, one by one,
At my pleasure I made slaughter,
So that none
E'er had time to look behind, or backward fled ;
Where he fell, did each one lay
On that day,
From the dust none ever lifted up his head.

Then the wretched king of Khita, he stood still,
With his warriors and his chariots all about him in a
      ring,
Just to gaze upon the valour of our king
In the fray.
And the king was all alone,
Of his men and chariots none
To help him; but the Hittite of his gazing soon had
      fill,
For he turned his face in flight, and sped away.
Then his princes forth he sent,
To battle with our lord,
Well equipped with bow and sword
And all goodly armament,

Chiefs of Leka, Masa, Kings of Malunna, Arathu,
Qar-qa-mash, of the Dardani, of Keshkesh, Khilibu.
And the brothers of the king were all gathered in one
    place,
Two thousand and five hundred pairs of horse—
And they came right on in force,
The fury of their faces to the flaming of my face.

Then, like Monthu in his might,
I rushed on them apace,
And I let them taste my hand
In a twinkling moment's space.
Then cried one unto his mate,
" This is no man, this is he,
This is Suteck, god of hate,
With Baal in his blood ;
Let us hasten, let us flee,
Let us save our souls from death,
Let us take to heel and try our lungs and breath."
And before the king's attack,
Hands fell, and limbs were slack,
They could neither aim the bow, nor thrust the
    spear,
But just looked at him who came
Charging on them, like a flame,
And the King was as a griffin in the rear.

(Behold thus speaks the Pharaoh, let all know),
" I struck them down, and there escaped me none.
Then I lifted up my voice, and I spake,
Ho ! my warriors, charioteers,
Away with craven fears,
Halt, stand, and courage take,
Behold I am alone,
Yet Ammon is my helper, and his hand is with me
    now."

When my Menna, charioteer, beheld in his dismay,
How the horses swarmed around us, lo ! his courage
    fled away,
And terror and affright
Took possession of him quite ;
And straightway he cried out to me, and said,
" Gracious lord and bravest king, saviour-guard
Of Egypt in the battle, be our ward ;
Behold we stand alone, in the hostile Hittite ring,
Save for us the breath of life,
Give deliverance from the strife,
Oh ! protect us, Ramses Miamun ! Oh ! save us,
    mighty King ! "

Then the King spake to his squire, " Halt ! take
    courage, charioteer,

As a sparrow-hawk swoops down upon his prey,
So I swoop upon the foe, and I will slay,
I will hew them into pieces, I will dash them into dust;
Have no fear,
Cast such evil thought away,
These godless men are wretches that in Ammon put
    no trust."
Then the king, he hurried forward, on the Hittite
    host he flew,
" For the sixth time that I charged them," says the
    king—and listen well,
" Like Baal in his strength, on their rearward, lo ! I
    fell,
And I killed them, none escaped me, and I slew, and
    slew, and slew."

CHAPTER VII.

THE OLDEST BOOK IN THE WORLD:
"THE PRECEPTS OF PTAH-HOTEP."

FIFTH DYNASTY, 3366–3266 B.C.

IT is, unfortunately, the custom nowadays, to look at the title of a book, and then to turn to its last pages; for the convenience of readers, the most important chapter of this little book, "Notes for the Nile," is therefore put last.

There is something very interesting in being able to read the oldest book in the world; thanks to the indefatigable labours of M. Philippe Virey, and to all who have helped him in his battle, against overwhelming difficulties in Egyptian philology, this is now possible for us.

The Prisse papyrus, discovered at Thebes, and now preserved in the Bibliothèque Nationale at Paris, is the oldest papyrus in the world. M. Chabas, who first made known the contents of this treatise, in his essay in the "Revue Archéologique" in 1857, described it as "Le plus ancien livre du monde," and, since the papyrus belongs to the eleventh dynasty, and was written about 2500 B.C., this is no overstatement; yet, old as the papyrus is, it contains but a copy of a much older treatise, written down by a certain viceroy or governor of Egypt, Patah-hotep or Ptah-hotep, or, according to later spelling, Ptah-hetep, the son of the seventh king of the fifth dynasty, Assa or Tet-ka-rā, who began to reign somewhere about the year 3366 B.C.

We have it from the lips of this old philosopher, Ptah-hotep, that these precepts were but a compilation, a gathering together of the sayings of the wise, that had been current probably for centuries before his time. So then, if we would have a glimpse at the ways and thoughts of men in the pyramid or pre-pyramid days, and would understand something of the moral and social code and condition of the people in the earliest historic times of the oldest civilisation whereof the world holds record, we must turn to the " Precepts of Ptah-hotep." If we wish to be wise with the most ancient wisdom of the Egyptians, we must thank the wise old prefect who, high in station, with 110 summers on his head, full of years, dignity and wisdom, determined to set down all the proverbs of his day, in rhythmic order and metrical arrangement, that so they might be the better remembered, from generation to generation.

Travellers to Egypt who visit the Gîzeh Museum will remember the tomb-monument of a contemporary Ptah-hotep. They will have noted the great, grey granite stele, brought from this old pluralist's grave, whereon may be seen upon the side lintels, the pictures of his four sons, for whose benefit they may, if they will, imagine that the prefect was moved to compile the "precepts." This older Ptah-hotep was a priest of the Pyramids of Aser, Ra-en-user and the "divine dwelling of Men-kau-Hor," and lived in the fifth dynasty.

As they gazed at the lintel-head they will have observed this pyramid-priest, Ptah-hotep, seated at the table of offerings, the "menu" of his repast carved on the stone behind him. Nor will they have omitted to visit the interesting tomb of the old priest itself, close to Mariette's house at Sakkarah.

But those who would understand more of the life and labour of the wise old prefect, whom we may piously imagine was related to the Ptah-hotep of Gîzeh Museum fame, and learn something of the kind of life he led when he was in the flesh, and when he was gathering together his proverbs more than 5000 years ago, will risk being bitten by the dog of the doorkeeper, and will make a point of inspecting the tomb of a prefect of later days, one Rechmarā, who was buried in the hot hillside of Abd El Kûrnah, above the Ramesseum, in a tomb, numbered to-day by Wilkinson (35) and by Champollion (25), and whose tomb-chambers, though woefully battered, are full of paintings and texts that illustrate the wisdom and life of Ptah-hotep.

This Rechmarā was prefect under Thothmes III., in the eighteenth dynasty, 1600 B.C.; but though 2000 years separate this time from the viceroyalty of Ptah-hotep, it is quite clear that the unchanging Egypt was little altered, and the duties and ethics of the prefect and magistrate in the time of Ptah-hotep the sage, when Assa was king, were much the same as they were when Thothmes III. was on the throne and Rechmarā was keeper of the royal granaries.

This "oldest book in the world," though it emphasises the fast-fading pictures upon the walls of Rechmarā's tomb, which may be said to be a kind of later illustrated edition of the work, has its chiefest interest for us, in being a handbook to the condition of thought and life and labour, of social and moral condition and code, in the centuries that span the gulf between the time of the Pyramids and the fifth dynasty, and the reign of the Antef and the eleventh dynasty kings.

Yet again, as we listen to Ptah-hotep, there come home to us echoes of a much later date than the date of the Antefs. Echoes of the Book of Job and Wisdom of Solomon—Whispers of the Hebraic decalogue. Such words as "Good words are more difficult to find

than the emerald ; " " If thou art a wise man bring up
thy son in the fear of God ; " " If any one beareth
himself proudly he will be humbled by God who
maketh his strength ; " " A dutiful son will have long
days in the land on that account ; " " A good son is
one of the gifts of God "—such words, from " the oldest
book in the world," irresistibly remind one of the best
book in the world to-day.   Joseph, in like position as
Ptah-hotep, may have got these precepts by heart.
Nor can one help the thought that Moses, learned in
all the wisdom of the Egyptians, would probably have
been made familiar with this ancient book of Egyptian
teaching, during his stay at the City of the Sun.

Turning to the precepts of Ptah-hotep, one is
not only touched by the simplicity and directness of
their teaching, but one feels their humanity.   We are
kinder to that old Egyptian dawn of history that needs
our kindness, because we feel we have one human
heart.

Thirty-three centuries may have passed since the
words were written ; but what can be more human
and powerful, in its appeal to right-mindedness, than
the following Precept xxx. :

" If thou become great, after thou hast been little, if
thou hast become rich after thou hast been poor, when
thou art at the head of the city, know well how to
use the position that thou hast gained.   Harden not
thy heart because of thy rank, remember that thou art

become only the steward of the good things of God. Put not behind thee thy neighbour who is as thou once wast. Treat him as an equal."

Throughout these " Precepts " one finds not only simplicity, directness, and high-mindedness, but great refinement.

Subjects that are very difficult to handle are dealt with, with the utmost delicacy. Indeed, it is possible that the entire absence of reference to death, or the dead, may have been just a piece of the good-breeding of the writer who knew the feeling of his time and his audience, on such matters.

This old-world Lord Chesterfield is addressing himself to an upper and educated class, and his appeal to the gentlemanly in man, is constant.

There are, it is clear, two distinct classes in the country—the governing and the governed. This it is felt is the Lord's doing, and men had better be content. But whilst instant obedience and fidelity are expected of the servant, the master is bound to be kind and considerate ; and if one belongs to the magistrate or the land-owning classes, magistrate and proprietor must realise that wealth and power imply duties, and lay great responsibilities upon those in whose hands the privilege lies.

Men who climb to high state, must be clothed with humility. Men in high estate must wear " the white flower of a blameless life," must be fearlessly just, be instant in protecting the fallen, and in seeing that the poor of the earth have right.

Charitableness, peaceableness and content, liberality, temperance, chastity, sobriety, energy in daily business, truthfulness, kindness, dutifulness and good temper, and calmness of mind—all these things are inculcated as being good for the souls of men and the nation's life, in the days of Assa the king; and one wonders whether the nineteenth century has found a more excellent way. It is nevertheless true that prudence, and not self-sacrifice and love, is the motive for the practical wisdom that is inculcated.

Ptah-hotep has some useful advice to give young men, in their treatment of young women. He has counsel to give the married men, in their treatment of their wives. But it is as an instructor of youth, and in his advice to fathers on the training up the child in the way it should go, that the old proverb-maker seems most in earnest.

The home was the foundation of society in his mind: the best school of duty and loyalty to king and country, was the family.

That he knew the ways of children and their memories, is evident from his determination to put his advice into metrical form, that so they might be preserved to posterity. One wishes one knew more of those old Egyptian metres. All that is probable is, that accent, not rhyme, was depended on to give true natural effect.

The emphasis laid by Ptah-hotep upon the need of accurate oral tradition, looks as if books, in his time, were scarce; yet it is clear, from reading the precepts, that wisdom and greatness were then synonymous terms—the truly wise ones were the truly great.

If we had any doubt as to the far-advanced condition of civilisation on the banks of the Nile in the year 3366 B.C., a peep at the precepts of Ptah-hotep, the Prince, would dispel it. A book that makes the Pyramid age possible to us; a book that fills the tombs of the fourth, fifth, and sixth dynasties with voices; that opens the diorite lips of Chephren, and sets the statues of Tih, Ra Nefer, Ra-hetep, Nefert, Ptah-hotep and the Shêk El Beled talking to us, and telling us of their thought and feeling, that makes the Salle de l'Ancien Empire, in the Gîzeh Museum, eloquent, is a book of proverbs, much to be thankful for.

This metrical rendering is based upon the English translation of M. Philippe Virey, published in the new series of " Records of the Past " (vol. iii. p. 16).

I have at times availed myself of the variorum readings and literal translations given in the footnotes, and where lacunæ occur, I have had to make a guess at the meaning from the context. This is notably the case with Precept XXXII.

The metre has been varied where possible to prevent weariness.   Blank verse has only been adopted where the matter seemed to demand it, and there, form has been sacrificed to the need of literal rendering.   Titles to the different precepts have been added for the convenience of the reader.

The sayings of Ptah-hotep himself, as opposed to those he collected and reduced to metre (xxxvii. to xliv.), have been indicated.

T

THE PRECEPTS OF PTAH-HOTEP.

3366–3266 B.C.

THE precepts of the prefect, feudal lord
Ptah-hotep, he who lived when Assa reigned,
Assa, the king of Egypt, north and south,
Assa, who lives to all eternity.

I.

Thus doth the feudal lord, Ptah-hotep, say,
" O god, whose feet are on the crocodiles,*
Osiris !   Man unto his dotage falls,
Decay comes on him, and his years decline,
Youth's glory fades; each day an old man's heart
Is vexed and wearied more ; his eyes go blind,
His ear grows deaf, and ceaselessly his strength

---

* It is believed that this is a reference to the 43rd invocation
of the 142nd chapter of " The Book of the Dead "—" O Osiris !
God of the two crocodiles ! "—but visitors to the Gîzeh Museum
will observe the beautiful stele of Horus on the crocodiles, " the
aged who becomes young in his hour, the old man who becomes
a child," and may draw their own inference.

Dissolves and dwindles, lo ! his mouth is dumb,
He speaks not as he spoke ; his feeble mind
Remembers not the deeds of yesterday.
Yea, his whole body suffers ; good is ill,
Taste disappears.   Ah, miserable man !
Age is thy misery, the nostrils cease
To drink the breath of heaven, the lungs grow weak,
To sit or stand is utter weariness.
Who then shall give my tongue authority
To tell the young the counsels from of old ?
What power will grant me sanction to declare
Counsels divine—the counsels heard from Heaven ?
Oh, God, permit me, send me double grace,
And let these evils be removed from them
Who are enlightened."
                                Answer makes the god :
" Instruct them in the counsels from of old,
For wisdom from of old it is that makes
The merit of the children of the great,
For that which gives equality of soul
Doth pierce the heart that hears it ; wisdom cries,
And of her voice is no satiety."

II^A.

Here doth begin the rhythmic ordering
Of those wise sayings spoken by the lord,
Father divine and well-beloved of God,
Son of the King, and first-born of his race

The prefect, hight Ptah-hotep, feudal lord,
Set down to give the ignorant and fools
A knowledge of each precept's argument.
To him who hears, these words are profitable;
To him who shall transgress them, endless loss:
Thus doth he speak, in counsel to his son.

II[B].

ON WISDOM AND HUMILITY.

Be not of your learning vain,
　　Treat the simple and the wise
　　With like honour.　Open lies
Art's great gate for all, and they
Who have entered by that way,
　　Know, how still before them flies
The perfection they would gain.
But wise sayings hidden are,
　　Like the emerald that is mined,
　　Or the hard-won gem, slaves find
Packed within the quartz and spar.

III.

ON DEALING WITH TEMPER.

If a man in a passion you meet,
　　And you know he is really your master,

Give way, nor get into a heat,
   Hands off, and so save a disaster.
He will stick to his version, my friend,
   Interruption is idle and wrong,
Keep cool, you will win in the end,
   Contradicted, just govern your tongue.

If you deal with a disputant hot,
   Be like one who refuses to stir,
When he rails and abuses, rail not!
   And so you will vanquish him, sir.
For the bystanders, hearing the din,
   Say—" The man who provoked, shows no fight,
Is the best of the two "—you will win,
   In the minds of the great, you are right.

IV.

ON KEEPING TEMPER.

   If a disputant you find
   In a rage, do not deride,
   For that you and he
   Cannot well agree,
   Take a different side;
   And because his mind

Differs, yea, though he be wrong,
Be not angered, rather fling
Far the thought of such a thing,
For consider well this matter,
How against himself, the tongue
Of a man in wrongful ire,
Fights, and wherefore still require
That your feelings he should flatter?
Never in the sight, take pleasure,
Of a man beyond control,
Though his rage amusing be,
He who does so, out of measure
Odious is of soul,
Mean and despicable he.
But beware of being moved
By your feelings, have good heed,
He who lets his feelings lead,
By the great one is reproved.

v.

ON LAW AND ORDER.

If, as a leader, thou art called to give
  Judgment on others, see thou take great care,
  So that thy conduct be esteemèd fair,
And strive without reproach, thyself to live.

Who hinders law, for violence makes way,
  No mob the upper hand can ever gain,
If justice on the judgment-seat remain,
And Right-is-might, not Might-is-right hath sway.

  The ends of justice change not, ever one
  In scope, so doth the father teach the son.

VI.

ON TRUE INFLUENCE.

Him, who tries to rule by dread,
  God in turn will rule by fright,
  He who boasts that fear, is might,
God will from his mouth take bread.

If a man through fear, be grown
  Wealthy, God will claim his land,
  If he boast a bully's hand,
God shall break the bully down.

God wills none should make afraid,
  Grant the people means to live
  Peacefully, they will regive
Toll, not grudged, but gladly paid.

VII.

ON MANNERS AT TABLE.

If it chance to a dinner you go
  At the house of a man that is great,
  Take that which is put on on your plate,
And bow, sir, exceedingly low.

Look well at whatever is placed
  In front, but don't point with the finger,
  Nor too long let your eyes on it linger,
For to stare, is not very good taste.

Do not bother your host with your chatter,
  For you never know quite what will please,
  If he speaks to you, be at your ease,
Talk away as you like, and no matter.

For the rich man, the great among men,
  Does just what he likes with his own,
  If he chooses he lays himself down
And goes off to sleep, there and then.

Just the wave of a hand, all is well
  All is done—if who waves it is great ;
  But God it is gives us our state,
Rich or poor, and we cannot rebel.

VIII.

On Errand-going.

If on any errand sent,
Be upon the thing intent,
Just as it was charged thee, ever
Certainly the charge deliver;
Alter not a single word,
Though it may offend my lord;
He who, just to please the ears
Of the man to whom he bears
Message, be he small or great,
From the truth one jot will bate,
Is a rogue we all must hate.

IX.

On Honest Dealing.

If you farm, reap the crops of your field
  Which the great god has given to till,
  Nor your mouth at your neighbour's house fill,
Better far the extortioner's yield.

In a little exaction, what harm?
　　But to steal, no! The man who is law
　　To himself, and with crocodile-jaw,
Will seize on his poor neighbour's farm—

His children we curse and we scorn;
　　His father, he grieves for his child,
　　His mother with sorrow goes wild;
Better far that no child had been born.

But the man of his tribe who is head,
　　Because that he always has trod
　　In probity's path, is as god;
They will follow wherever he tread.

X.

ON KEEPING ONE'S PLACE.

If, in obedience to your master's will,
You evil do, the gods will think no ill.
And once you know who master is, who slave,
Then keep your place; respectfully behave,
Considering where respect is justly due,
And who has full authority o'er you.

Whether good fortune come, or bad betide,
Is fortune's law, caprice her only guide.
But he who treats his servants ill, will find
That God who gave him power to rule his kind,
Will in a moment turn from him, and lo!
Great is the one-time great man's overthrow.

XI.

ON ACTIVITY IN BUSINESS.

Be active, be up and be doing,
   Yea more than your master had bidden,
For the indolent comes but to ruin,
   The man who wastes time should be chidden.

Never lose any chance of increasing
   The goods that your household possesses,
Business grows—with your energy ceasing,
   There will cease too, the income that blesses.

XII.

ON TRAINING UP A CHILD IN THE WAY HE SHOULD GO.

If thou art wise, then train thy child to be
Devout, well-pleasing unto God, and see

If he conform his conduct to thy way
And does his duty, that thy love repay;
Flesh of thy flesh, and of thy bone a bone,
Ne'er let thy heart be separate from thy son;
But if he misbehave, transgress thy will,
Reject thy counsel, and advised by ill,
Run counter to thy wishes, then be stern,
And strike the mouth that struck thee, in return.
Instant commands for him who does not well
Is best, so shalt thou turbulent temper quell,
So from his duty's path he shall not stray,
And nothing mar the tenor of his way.

XIII.

On Store-Keeping.

Stand, sit, but do not fuss and walk about,
   If you are keeper of a Public Store,*

---

* The Public Store, or "Larit," here spoken of, was the
strongly-walled enclosure into which was brought the contribu-
tions of corn, by the taxpayer for public use in time of famine
Cf. Gen. xlvii. 24. The tax was heavy. When men paid of their
crop as they did to Joseph, there would be wry faces, hence Precept xxxiv. The Prefect alone had the key of the Larit. It
was one of his most most onerous duties to superintend the filling
and guarding of the store. Travellers should study the picture
of Filling the Larit on Rechmarā's tomb, at Thebes.

And make this rule, you never will be out,
   Absent, off duty, yea though wearied sore.

If any entering would communicate
   Secrets, keep eyes on him, and him suspect ;
Your trust is more than most appreciate,
   All argument against its worth, reject.

Know this, where unrelaxing rule is made,
   One for the privileged classes and the poor,
A god alone the storehouse can invade,
   But God will enter at that Granary door.

XIV.

ON SELF-MASTERY.

If it chance that with people you are,
   Who appear to be deeply in love,
Saying, " Soul of my soul, my life's star,
   What cure can my passion remove ?
Whatever thy heart says, let it be
   On the instant spontaneously done,
Sovereign master I yield unto thee,
   Thy opinion and mine, are as one.

" Thy name without speech, is approved,
   Thy body with vigour doth shine,

Oh face of all faces, beloved,
  More than all is the face that is thine."
Then I know, used to flattery, sir,
  If aught cross thy desire on its way,
There's an impulse within thee will stir,
  Its passion thy heart will obey.

But remember the man who gives in
  To passion's caprice and its call,
His soul is the servant of sin,
  His body to death is in thrall.
But he who is lord of his soul,
  Lives more than a god-gifted life,
While the man, whom his passions control,
  Is under the sway of his wife.

XV.

On Honest Speech.

Declare thy line, have done with reticence,
  Yea, even in the council of thy lord
    Speak out thy mind, let others backward go,
  And in their speeches swallow their own word,
Lest peradventure they should give offence,
  Be not as they, nor feign, nor answer, so

Saying, " My friends the man who plain can see,
   How wrong the rest are, he alone is wise,
     And when the great wise man doth deign oppose
   Error, and lift his voice, make no replies,
Rather let all be silent after me,
   Surely the great and wise man only, knows."

XVI.

ON TRUE TEACHING.

If thou a teacher be,
Set forth thy plan,
As thou decidest, see
Thou play the man.

Do what is good and just,
Perfect, complete ;
Deeds that when thou art dust,
Still shall be sweet.

Never let words decide,
Flattery disdain,
Words such as foster pride
Words that make vain.

XVII.

ON THE BENCH.

If e'er thou art a Justice of the Peace,
　　Hear all the poor petitioner will say,
Be not abrupt, but set him at his ease,
　　Nor cry, " You've said that twenty times,
　　　　away ! "

Indulgent be, so shalt thou give him heart,
　　And he the object of his suit will gain,
Better he tell what led unto his smart,
　　Than that he wearily describe his pain.

Be not abrupt with him who comes to law,
　　To disentangle evidence, be kind,
Abruptness closes the complainant's jaw,
　　Patience alone will open all his mind.

XVIII.

ON FALSE LOVE.

Do you wish, sir, respect should be paid
　　In the house of your master—the home
　　　　Of your friend, or where'er you may be ;
　　Then beware, and, on entering, see

That you make no advance to the maid,
  No good of such courting can come.

For the man who takes part in that game
  Is a madman ; what thousands destroy
    Themselves, and contentedly seem
    To risk all for a shadowy dream,
For a moment of pleasure, win shame,
  And death, bitter death for the joy !

The villain who, lust all afire,
  Of set purpose to flirting will fall,
    If his end to its end he pursue,
    Lo ! his mind will abandon him too ;
He who does not contemn such desire,
  Scorn such act, has no senses at all.

XIX.

ON BAD HUMOUR.

If an even course and good,
  You desire, from evil free,
Keep from an ill-humoured mood,
  All attacks of temper flee,
He who enters to that mind,
No repose on earth will find.

U

Evil humour discord makes,
　'Twixt the father and the mother,
Bond 'twixt wife and husband breaks,
　Sets the girl against her brother;
Unto it all sins belong,
All embodiments of wrong.

He who with a wise man's will,
　In just balance of his thought,
Weighs the worth of good or ill,
　Walks thereafter as he ought,
Such, where'er he chance to rest,
Never finds ill-temper, guest.

XX.

On Irritability.

Keep your temper, grumble not,
With your neighbour be not cross,
Speak not rudely, oil your tongue,
Compliment is gain, not loss;
He who prone to passion hot,
Of his words no longer master,
At his neighbour raves, is wrong.
Let not trifles irritate,
Being vexed, you but create
Sorrow, that is sure to stay,
When the pet has passed away.

XXI.

On Conjugal Felicity.

If thou art wise, of things at home beware,
    Love thou thy wife, and love her without lack,
    Fill thou her stomach well, well clothe her back,
This for her person is the chiefest care.

See that her ointments fail not, and caress her,
    Each day she lives, her heart's desire fulfil,
    For know, that honouring his lady's will
In kindness, honours him who doth possess her.

Never be brutal, or brute violence use,
    Tact, it is tact will influence her desires,
    Think what she aims at, and to what aspires,
What she regards, and what she most would choose.

This is the way to keep her heart at home,
    Repel her,—lo ! a gulf between you grows !
    Call her, display thy love, she sees and knows,
Open thine arms, she to thine arms will come.

XXII.

On Kindness to Dependents.

Treat well your dependents, if able, for Heaven
    Who granted position, gave power to do it,

And he, who no grace to his servants has given,
  Is a fool, as the proverb says, certain to rue it.

For who of us knows what to-morrow may bring him;
  He is wise and well-balanced of heart, who is kind
To dependents, if ever hard fate try to fling him
  And he's put to a push, then the good he will find.

For then the retainers he kindly entreated,
  Will cry out, " Come on, let us help all we can."
But if e'er from the household, kind feeling has fleeted,
  They will fail at his need, and then woe to the man !

XXIII.

On Just Hearing and Speaking.

When men you hear extravagantly talking,
  Do not repeat their words, nor pay them heed,
  For swelling words from hasty mouths proceed ;
And if repeated, when abroad you're walking,
  Look on the ground, say nothing, and proceed.

Just be your speech, and speaking justly, cause
  Provokers to injustice, truth to know ;
  Just be your deed, let all to Justice bow,
But to condemn things hateful to the laws,
  'Twere best from off their face the veil to throw.

XXIV.

ON PUBLIC SPEAKING.

If thou a wise man art, and chance to sit
　　Within the council-chamber of thy lord,
See that thou bend thy thought to what is fit,
　　Be silent, not too prodigal of word.

And when thou speakest, know the argument
　　Counter to thine.　To speak in public well
Is art, on which all critics are intent,
　　And contradiction best its worth can tell.

XXV.

ON COMMAND AND SELF-COMMAND.

　　If thou art great and strong,
　　Knowledge and calm of tongue
　　Hold in thy chief esteem.
　　Order, but with command
　　Show the directing hand ;
　　Never dictator seem,
　　Hectoring's wrong !

　　Be not proud-hearted, vain,
　　Meanness of soul disdain ;

Speak out thine orders, see
Thine answers penetrate ;
Keep coolness in debate,
And on thy face, let be
Gravity plain.

Don't burn thyself away,
Gentleness wins the day,
Fuss can't enjoy the sun,
Idlers let fortune slip ;
Don't overload the ship !
Sit thou ! let others run,
Others obey !

XXVI.

ON THE SECRETS OF SUCCESS IN WORK.

Never disturb a man on business bent,
Nor with distraction weaken his intent,
His task, not you, he to his arms would take,
Who turns his sleeves up for his labour's sake ;
Love for the work in hand is passport given,
To wing the souls of human kind to Heaven.
But be composed in trouble, smile on fate,
Let peace be yours when others agitate ;
For they who labour with unruffled calm,
These men succeed, they carry off the palm

XXVII.

On Tax Gathering.

Teach men to the ruler due homage to tender,
If you gather the taxes, the tax in full, render
To him by whose bounty you live ;
But, believe me, the gift of your master's affection
Is more than all food and the ample protection
For your back, that his favour can give.

For the tax he receives, to your household is able
To grant, without question, good lodging, good table,
And all things that your station requires ;
A beneficent hand can the master extend,
And add to your goods things more good, without end,
By the tax at your hand, he acquires.
Your love in the hearts of who love you instil,
And let loving obedience wait on your will.

XXVIII.

On Taking Orders.

Are you enrolled a member of police,
Son of the guardian of our public peace,
Then, though the why you may not understand,
Your duty do, with firmness give command.

Fulfil instructions just as they were sent,
And mind the words, not what you think was meant ;
The master knows why so the order ran,
Yours not to comment, you are message-man.

XXIX.

On Avoiding the Disagreeable.

Friend, if anything displease,
And, though acting in his right,
   Anyone should tease,
Get away from out his sight
When he ceases to address thee,
Think not how he did distress thee,
   And forget his spite.

XXX.

On Humility in High Estate.

If after being little thou art great,
   And riches after poverty hast gained,
When thou art come unto the ruler's state,
   Know how to use the rank thou hast attained.

Let not thine heart be hardened by high place,
   Think, these good things God doth to thee but lend,
Put not thy one-time neighbour from thy face,
   Be still, to him, as equal and a friend.

XXXI.

On Content at Court.

Bend thou thy back before the greater lord,
For see,
Once get to Court, thy fortune, bed and board,
Are bound up with the king's prosperity,
And to thy station shall thy gains accord.

But this remember, that in high estate,
Annoy
Comes to the man who finds some one more great
Put o'er his head, he seems to lose his joy,
Vexation daily doth this thing create.

It cannot harm thy soul, though it may tease
To hear,
" Shame ! do not rob your neighbour's house, nor
    seize
By violence the goods that may be near ! "
Exclaim not, nor be hurt by words like these.

Nay, keep thy temper, and though hindered sore
Thou be,
Remember, he who heavy on thee bore,
Is bowed himself beneath authority,
And, in his turn, will feel its weight the more.

XXXII.

On Hidden Sorrow.

Do not make mischief, water from the well
  Runs only down the trench a certain way,
But, having sunk, none can its secrets tell,
  And in the earth's deep bosom it must stay.
Let it not be that having dealt a smart,
You leave the wrong to rankle in the heart.

XXXIII.

On Courtesy in Conversation.

If a gentleman's manners are yours,
  Do not shout your friend's name when you meet,
Nor talk what annoys him or bores,
  But see that the subject is sweet.

Do not rush to discussions at once,
   To his mind let the matter first sink,
And give him good time, for the nonce,
   On the gist of the question to think.

If his ignorance come to the fore,
   And he puts himself quite in your hand,
With courtesy treat him the more,
   Do not corner your friend, I command.

Never taunt him with words of reproach,
   Nor answer him crushingly, so
Again he the subject may broach,
   And more wise for your talk he will go.

XXXIV.

ON WEARING A CHEERFUL COUNTENANCE.

Wear a look of contentment and pleasure!
   When we see a man leaving the Store,
Who has come to contribute his measure
   Of corn, with a face, sick and sore—

His stomach is empty, it's plain, sir,
   By that look when he went on his way,
To rebel at our laws he is fain, sir,
   Beware his example, I say.

XXXV.

On True Worthiness.

Remember those who faithful to thee proved,
  When thou wast poor and of but low degree,
Then for thine honest merit wast thou loved,
  Thy worth was more than those who honoured thee.

True worth is what a man's heart doth possess
  Entire, completely, as none other can,
More than his rank is honest worthiness,
  This stays, that passes on from man to man.

A child's good merit profiteth his father,
  A sire his own son's worthiness may thank,
But what the young man is, we honour rather,
  Than mere remembrance of the father's rank.

XXXVI.

On Wise Discrimination.

The master-man who doth direct the toil
  Of those who labour, honour him the most!
Whose hand is soft, and little used to soil,
  He is the gentleman ; to higher post
Who climbs, and having climbed, would keep his station,
Let him beware of insubordination.

XXXVII.

ON WIFE MANAGEMENT.

If you wed, to wife be kind,
Do not cross her, let her mind,
  More than all her fellows, be content.
For the wife who finds her bond
Pleasant, will be doubly fond.
Do not e'er repel a wife,
Grant her anything in life;
In her own contentment's state,
She will best appreciate
  All that your sweet love's direction meant.

XXXVIII.

PTAH-HOTEP SOLILOQUISES.

These are the sayings that I counsel thee,
Hear them, and in thy mind shall wisdom be
Fully advanced; yet, though they are the means
Whereby all justice and all truth shall reign,
And therefore are they precious, still would fade
Remembrance of them from the lips of men,
But, thanks unto my careful ordering
And rhythmical arrangement, all these words

Will now, unaltered over all the earth,
Eternally be carried.   They will serve
As texts to be embellished, annotated,
Whereof the great will speak, and in the schools
Philosophers instruct men in their sayings.
The scholar having listened, will become
A master-workman, yea, because he listened
With close attention when he heard these words.
So let him by their means first rank attain,
Position perfect, to endure for ever,
Place, beyond which he nothing can desire.
For lo, by knowledge is his path assured,
By knowledge is he happy on the earth,
By knowledge has his soul satiety,
He feels by his own merit, he is great.
His mind and mouth completely in accord,
Just are his words, his eyes with justice see,
And justly can he hear, and lo his son
Does justice, through these sayings, undeceived.

XXXIX.

PTAH-HOTEP ON ATTENTION TO PRECEPT.

Attend to precepts ! it is profitable
Unto the son of him who has attended !

From listening well the power of listening grows,
Fit audience forms the óne-time auditor.
Good, when he has attended, when he speaks,
Good also, he who listened well has gained,
And we shall gain by listening unto him.
Attention more than anything is worth,
For it produces love, the one good thing
That is twice good.   The son, who doth accept
The instruction of his father, will grow old,
Long in the land his days, on that account;
For what God loves is that one should attend,
If one attends not, that doth God abhor.
For see, the heart is master to itself,
Attends, or doth not, at its own sweet will,
But if it do attend, then to a man,
His heart is master most beneficent.
Attending to instruction has reward,
For what he gives his mind to, a man loves,
And doing that which is for him prescribed
Finds pleasure.   And it is a two-fold joy
When that a son attends unto his father,
For then if wise things are prescribed to him,
The son is gentle-minded towards his master,
Attending to the man who, in his turn,
Attended to like things, prescribed to him.
Well doth the son engrave upon his heart,
Wise sayings that his father has approved;
For so the recollection of it runs,

Preserved in precept, on from mouth to mouth
Of those, who have their being upon earth.

XL.

PTAH-HOTEP ON HOME EDUCATION.

Happy the sons whom fathers educate,
There is no error in their being's plan ;
Train thou thy son to be a docile man,
Whose wisdom is agreeable to the great ;
Let him direct his mouth by what is said,
Docility his wisdom doth discover ;
Conduct in him grows perfect, day by day,
While error casts the unteachable away ;
The ignorant and fool will be thrown over,
But knowledge shall lift up the scholar's head.

XLI.

PTAH-HOTEP ON THE UNTEACHABLE AND FOOLS.

As for the man who lacks experience
And listens not, he nothing good can do.
Knowledge he seems to see in ignorance,
Profit in loss—to mischief he will go,

And running in the error of his ways,
Chooses the opposite of what men praise;
And so on what is perishing he lives,
With evil words his belly he doth fill,
Yea, thereat is astonied, and he thrives
On what great men think vain, shortlived, and ill,
And daily from things profitable flies,
Misled by errors' multiplicities.

XLII.

Ptah-Hotep on Teaching.

Blest the son who doth attend,
He—a follower of Horus—
Rises ever to his end,
And in greatness goes before us,
He unto his children gives
Precepts sure, by which he lives.

On his father's precepts, none
Ere should dare to innovate,
Let us teach unto the son
What our father did dictate,
So the children shall declare
" Wonderful thy precepts are."

X

Cause thou justice then to flourish,
Where thy sons their learning take,
Justice so their souls will nourish ;
But if teachers truth forsake,
Witless ones who hear them teach,
Will but follow in their speech.

Docile folk, to their disaster,
Do what teachers say they must,
All the world cries, " Here's a master,"
And the public give their trust ;
But much sooner than will please
Lo their fame and glory cease.

Of these ancient sayings, brother,
Add no word nor take away,
Put not one thing for another ;
Hidden in thine heart must stay
Rebel thoughts that will arise ;
Teach the sayings of the wise.

Listen thou, if thou wouldst dwell
In the mouth of those who hear thee ;
In thy teacher's office—well
They who listen will revere thee,
Hang upon thy lips, and know
That from a master's chair, thy wit and
    wisdom flow.

XLIII.

Ptah-hotep on Obedience to Masters.

Think much, but never let thy mouth run on,
Then shalt thou argue with the great and wise,
But put thyself in union with the way
Of him thy master, so that when he cries
" This is my child "—then those that hear shall say,
" Blest be the mother of so good a son ! "
Unto thy speech thy soul of souls apply,
Speak perfect things, or speak thou not at all,
So shall the great who listen to thee, cry,
" Twice good is that which from his lips doth fall."

XLIV.

Ptah-hotep on Obedience to Fathers— His Last Word.

Do as your master bids you, how much rather
Know thou, my son, the precepts of thy father,
Get his commands by heart, to please, his will,
Beyond the letter of his word, fulfil,
Truly the gift of God is a good son
Who doth more than was ordered to be done.

He strives to satisfy his master's heart,
With all his might doth choose the better part.
So shall thy body healthful be, thy king
Will be content with thee in everything.
Upon thee many days the sun shall shine,
And length of years without default be thine.
Wisdom has caused me, in high place, to live
Long on the earth, a hundred years and ten,
I found the favour that a king can give,
First, for life's labour, honoured amongst men.*

---

* Colophon—It is finished, from its beginning to its end, according to that which is found in writing.